POETRY alive

PERSPECTIVES

POETRY *alive*

PERSPECTIVES

COMPILED AND EDITED BY

Dom Saliani
Calgary Board of Education

Copp Clark Pitman Ltd.
A Longman Company

Toronto

ILLUSTRATION:
Renée Cuthbertson: 127, 166
Kyle Gell: 1, 45, 59, 77, 117, 126, 151, 156, 183
Christopher Griffin: 27, 112, 158, 202
Stuart Knox: 24, 31, 57, 89, 108
Monika Laskowski: 17, 63, 97, 137, 169, 206
Susan Leopold: 3, 13, 41, 94, 100, 113
Steve MacEachern: 8, 29, 65, 87, 103
Allan Moon: 28, 114, 160, 197
Liz Nyman: 38, 82, 164

ISBN 0-7730-5147-3

EDITING: **Muriel Napier**
DESIGN: **Jo-Anne Slauenwhite**
COVER DESIGN AND ILLUSTRATION: **Sharon Matthews**
TYPESETTING: **Compeer Typographic Services Limited**
PRINTING AND BINDING: **Webcom**
The compiler would like to acknowledge John McAllister and Larry Liffiton for their contributions.

Canadian Cataloguing in Publication Data

Main entry under title:

Poetry alive : perspectives

Includes index.
ISBN 0-7730-5147-3

1. Canadian poetry (English).* 2. English poetry.
3. American poetry. 4. English poetry –
Translations from foreign languages. I. Saliani, Dom.

PS8279.P62 1991 821.008 C91-093761-3
PR9195.25.P62 1991

Printed and bound in Canada

8 9 10 WC 02 01 00

CONTENTS

1 THE POET'S EYE

The poet's eye, in a fine frenzy rolling,
Doth glance from heaven to earth, from earth to heaven;
And as imagination bodies forth
The forms of things unknown . . .

2 WHEN UNICORNS WERE STILL POSSIBLE

When I was young, it seemed that life was so wonderful,
a miracle, oh it was beautiful, magical.
And all the birds in the trees, well they'd be singing so happily,
joyfully, playfully, watching me.

3 ON THE WAY TO SCHOOL

On the way to school
One morning long ago
I stopped to look at the sunrise . . .

4 NOTHING GOLD CAN STAY

But pleasures are like poppies spread—
You seize the flow'r, its bloom is shed;
Or like the snow falls in the river—
A moment white—then melts for ever.

5 A LOVER'S EYES

A lover's eyes will gaze an eagle blind,
A lover's ear will hear the lowest sound . . .
Love's feeling is more soft and sensible
Than art the tender horns of cockled snails . . .
For valour, is not Love a Hercules? . . .
Never durst poet touch a pen to write
Until his ink were temp'red with love's sighs.

6 THE PAIN OF EARTH-BOUND THINGS

The world of dew
Is the world of dew,
And yet . . .
And yet . . .

7 High Flight and Dark Conclusions

There are two types of realists—
the one who offers a good deal of dirt with his potato,
to show that it is a real one;
and the one who is satisfied with the potato brushed clean.

8 LETTERS TO A FUTURE GENERATION

Above all I am not concerned with Poetry.
My subject is War, and the pity of War.
The Poetry is in the pity.

9 LET'S SKIP TRUTH TODAY

If you are a dreamer, come in,
If you are a dreamer, a wisher, a liar,
A hope-er, a pray-er, a magic bean buyer . . .
If you're a pretender, come sit by my fire
For we have some flax-golden tales to spin.
Come in!
Come in!

10 PROMISES TO KEEP

I go to encounter for the millionth time
the reality of experience
and to forge in the smithy of my soul
the uncreated conscience of my race

11 TO SEE THE EARTH AS IT TRULY IS

To see the earth as it truly is—
small and blue and beautiful in that
eternal silence where it floats, is to see
ourselves as riders on the earth together.

12 Here Comes the Sun

Give me the splendid silent sun with all its beams full-dazzling,
Give me juicy autumnal fruit ripe and red from the orchard,
Give me a field where the unmow'd grass grows . . .
Give me a garden of beautiful flowers where I can walk undisturb'd.

Chapter One

1 The Poet's Eye

The poet's eye, in a fine frenzy rolling,
Doth glance from heaven to earth, from earth to heaven;
And as imagination bodies forth
The forms of things unknown . . .

from A Midsummer Night's Dream

WILLIAM SHAKESPEARE

2

POETS AND POETRY

Most of us, at one time or another, have tried writing poetry. We recognize that through poetry we can express thoughts and feelings that would otherwise leave us tongue-tied.

Some poems we read touch us deeply, others startle and amuse us with their insight and cleverness. Some may even present us with information that changes our views and attitudes.

A poet sees the world through very special eyes. This sensitivity, combined with an unrelenting love of language, results in poetry.

The poems in this chapter explore the nature of poetry and the characteristics of the poet. What is poetry? Can it be defined? How relevant is poetry in our lives? What is a poet? Why do poets write? How important is the relationship between the poet and reader?

Poetry is to prose as dancing is to walking.
JOHN WAIN

Poetry is the opening and closing of a door,
leaving those who look through to guess about
what is seen during a moment.
CARL SANDBURG

Poetry is the impish attempt to paint the colour
of the wind.
MAXWELL BODENHEIM

Poetry is nothing but healthy speech.
HENRY DAVID THOREAU

I did not decide to become a poet—I was
always writing poetry.
E.E. CUMMINGS

Between what I see and what I say,
between what I say and what I keep silent,
between what I keep silent and what I dream,
between what I dream and what I forget:
poetry.
OCTAVIO PAZ

CONVERSATION WITH A POET

MIROSLAV HOLUB
(translated by Ewald Osers)

Are you a poet?
  Yes, I am.
How do you know?
  I've written poems.
If you've written poems it means you *were* a poet. But now?
  I'll write a poem again one day.
In that case maybe you'll be a poet again one day. But how will you know it is a poem?
  It will be a poem just like the last one.
Then of course it won't be a poem. A poem is only once and can never be the same a second time.
  I believe it will be just as good.
How can you be sure? Even the quality of a poem is for once only and depends not on you but on circumstances.
  I believe that circumstances will be the same too.
If you believe that then you won't be a poet and never were a poet. What then makes you think you are a poet?
  Well—I don't rightly know. And who are you?

Assignment: Poetry

KAYLA L. McCLURG

I never see anything to write a poem about,
you say.
Statement. Matter-of-fact and sure.

But look!
There in the corner
spying out at you through the knotholes
the king of woodwork keeps sullen watch
and beneath him, suspiciously silent,
lintballs gather to ravage the room by night.
There, there is a poem.

Behind you (listen) a girl sighs
and lays down her head,
mingling black shiny strands
with green swirls on paper.
Texture and design and colour, one desk away.
There, there is a poem.

See the stacks of magazines,
how they lean to the east,
never falling
just threatening, threatening,
holding on by one thin whisper.
And the clock merely hums,
an adding machine tallying up our days.
There, too, is a poem.

Renegade hallway voices whip in and out,
a spear of sunlight ricochets off your watch
and into your eyes, while far away
typewriters and telephones administrate our lives,
and somewhere a class laughs
(in harmony, musical and rhythmic).

The whole building sways and swells with poetry,
waiting, waiting, waiting—
like the magazines,
like the girl behind you,
like the silent watching eyes—
waiting to be found.

Look at your world,
at what others do not see.
Wrap it in words,
and you will have a poem.

MARCI RIDLON

Man, I don't wanna write no poem.
I mean, likc, what's ta say?
Should I say, maybe, that Mrs. Perez
always smells of garlic
or that her kids
run up and down the halls
screamin'
till I think I'm gonna find me
the elevator shaft
and jump right in?
Ha, ha. How about this?
"The house is dirty,
the halls is dirty,
the street is dirty,
I'm dirty."
Pretty good, huh?
Or maybe you'd like me to
write down that
I'm getting pretty sick of
talkin' to you
and that I just don't feel
like writin' down nothing.
I ain't got nothing pretty ta say.
A poem's gotta be pretty, ain't it?

I Feel (Vers Libre)

LUCY MAUD MONTGOMERY

I feel
Very much
Like taking
Its unholy perpetrators
By the hair
Of their heads
(If they have any hair)
And dragging them around
A few times,
And then cutting them
Into small, irregular pieces
And burying them
In the depths of the blue sea.
They are without form
And void,/Or at least
The stuff they/produce
Is./They are too lazy
To hunt up rhymes;
And that
Is all
That is the matter with them.

Balance

SUSAN ZIMMERMAN

I must have written three poems
comparing life to wine vinegar
before my mother brought some home.

It wasn't what I'd expected.
It wasn't at all like life.

This is a service by mothers:
you write too much of deserts
and they threaten to send you there.

READING POETRY

MARY McIVER

I read a poem the way I eat
raspberries, pop the whole thing in and flip
the temporarily velvet bit over on my tongue
and enjoy picking the seeds out of my teeth later

or baked potatoes too hot, my mouth burning
and juggling the scalding bites

or the bitter fruit that has a necessarily
sweet nut at the core.

I read a poem the way I dream I fall off cliffs,
waiting for the shock as I hit.

I read a poem like one who has forgotten how to come up for air
who stays under the water in the deep quarry
exploring the ledges and granite blocks
that wish they had become part of banks or curbstones.

I read a poem the way I look for stones on the beach
one day it's the black smooth ovals with a bit
of a flaw that catch my eye. The next day it's
the flash of mica.

I read poems the way I remember dreams, unsure why they woke me,
wanting to dream them again.

I read poems the way I breathe, the way I never could dance,
the way I rode my bike on Rock County flatland trying
to get lost,
the way I listen for birds in the woods and try
to imagine how they look,
the way I wish I could swim, trusting the world,
the way I ran as a child pell mell downhill arms out
each foot miraculously falling right.

POETI-C ART

ARUDRA (BHAGAVATULA SANKARA SASTRI)
(translated by B.V.L. Narayana Row)

The poetic cart
has two wheels
equal
and efficient

what to say
and how

neither
is superior
to the other

if either one
is missing
there is
no cart
moving

GREATNESS

ALDEN NOWLAN

I would be the greatest poet the world has ever known
if only I could make you see
here on the page
sunlight
a sparrow
three kernels of popcorn
spilled on the snow.

YOU HAVE TWO VOICES

NANCY PRASAD

You have two voices when you speak
in English or your mother tongue.
When you speak the way your people spoke
the words don't hesitate but flow
like rivers, like rapids, like oceans of sound,
and your hands move like birds through the air.

But then you take a stranger's voice
when you speak in your new tongue.
Each word is a stone dropped in a pool.
I watch the ripples and wait for more.
You search in vain for other stones to throw.
They are heavy. Your hands hang down.

You have two voices when you speak;
I have two ears for hearing.
Speak to me again in your mother tongue.
What does it matter how little I understand
when the words pour out like music
and your face glows like a flame.

MOTIONLESS SWAYING

YANNIS RITSOS
(translated by Nikos Stangos)

As she jumped up to open the door,
she dropped the basket with the spools of thread—
they scattered under the table, under the chairs,
in improbable corners—one that was orange-red
got inside the lamp glass; a mauve one
deep in the mirror; that gold one—
she never had a spool of gold thread—where did it come from?
She was about to kneel, to pick them up one by one, to tidy up
before opening the door. She had no time. They knocked
again.
She stood motionless, helpless, her hands dropped to her sides.
When she remembered to open—no one was there.

Is that how it is with poetry, then? Is this exactly how it is
with poetry?

LISTEN, REAL POETRY DOESN'T SAY ANYTHING

JIM MORRISON

Listen, real poetry doesn't say anything, it just ticks off the possibilities. Opens all doors. You can walk through any one that suits you.

. . . and that's why poetry appeals to me so much—because it's so eternal. As long as there are people, they can remember words and combinations of words. Nothing else can survive a holocaust but poetry and songs. No one can remember an entire novel. No one can describe a film, a piece of sculpture, a painting, but so long as there are human beings, songs and poetry can continue.

If my poetry aims to achieve anything, it's to deliver people from the limited ways in which they see and feel.

from FOR E.J.P.

LEONARD COHEN

I once believed a single line
in a Chinese poem could change
forever how blossoms fell

TENTATIVE DEFINITIONS OF POETRY

CARL SANDBURG

1. Poetry is a projection across silences of cadences arranged to break that silence with definite intentions of echoes, syllables, wave lengths.
2. Poetry is the journal of a sea animal living on land, wanting to fly the air.
3. Poetry is a series of explanations of life, fading off into horizons too swift for explanations.
4. Poetry is a search for syllables to shoot at the barriers of the unknown and the unknowable.
5. Poetry is a theorem of a yellow-silk hankerchief knotted with riddles, sealed in a balloon tied to the tail of a kite flying in a white wind against a blue sky in spring.
6. Poetry is the silence and speech between a wet struggling root of a flower and a sunlit blossom of that flower.
7. Poetry is the harnessing of the paradox of earth cradling life and then entombing it.
8. Poetry is a phantom script telling how rainbows are made and why they go away.
9. Poetry is the synthesis of hyacinths and biscuits.
10. Poetry is the opening and closing of a door, leaving those who look through to guess about what is seen during a moment.

▲

''Poetry is when words sing''—six year old boy.
R. MURRAY SCHAFER (from *When Words Sing*)

Prose is the kind of writing everybody understands,
poetry is the other kind.
LOUIS DUDEK (from *Epigrams*)

How Beautifully Useless

RAYMOND SOUSTER

How beautifully useless,
how deliciously defiant
a poem is!

What Is the Validity of Your Life?

DOROTHY LIVESAY

The validity of my life
is a few poems caught and netted
a few strong feelings
about love and dying
and loss—
a few tempestuous cloudbursts
because people couldn't be
as great as they might have been
if they'd never learned
to play games—
a few doubts
about my own importance—
a delight   delighting in
puffed redbreast on a tree
eyeing me   and his mate
and the crows in the jack pine squawking
because there's a small grey cat
on the garage roof
spitting at them.

The validity of my life
is whether you read this poem
or not
and whether it speeds
your arrow.

THE SECRET

DENISE LEVERTOV

Two girls discover
the secret of life
in a sudden line of
poetry.

I who don't know the
secret wrote
the line. They
told me

(through a third person)
they had found it
but not what it was
not even

what line it was. No doubt
by now, more than a week
later, they have forgotten
the secret,

the line, the name of
the poem. I love them
for finding what
I can't find,

and for loving me
for the line I wrote,
and for forgetting it
so that

a thousand times, till death
finds them, they may
discover it again, in other
lines

in other
happenings. And for
wanting to know it,
for

assuming there is
such a secret, yes,
for that
most of all.

from A FEW NOTES ON POETRY

MARGARET ATWOOD

- I don't believe poetry is or should be "self-expression" in any narrow personal sense. Rather I see it as a condensing lens through which the human universe can see itself, an aural focussing through which human languages can hear themselves.
- Poems are made of words as paintings are made of paint. To bypass the words, the texture of a poem, in favour of "image," "theme" or "idea" is to neglect a poem's physicality in favour of some abstraction. To concentrate only on the verbal texture, though, is to ignore the nature of words themselves, since images, themes and ideas inhere in them. There is no such thing as a nonsense poem, if by that it's meant a collection of syllables that suggest nothing.
- A poem is completed not by the writer—who goes as far as she can, granted—but by the reader; which is to say, it is never fully completed, since each reader and therefore each reading is different.
- A poem that uses language or image in a new or unexpected way causes the electrical impulses in the brain to jump their habitual paths and form new synaptical connections. Those who revel in language enjoy this sensation. Those who would rather have their synapses stroked in familiar directions prefer highly conventional modes of literature. If you like having your synapses stroked, you should probably avoid poetry, especially modern poetry. Though it too has its conventions.

Conversation with a Poet/*Miroslav Holub/p. 3*
Rewrite the conversation to be just as meaningful by substituting another occupation for "poet" in the first line. Make any other changes you think are necessary.

Assignment: Poetry/*Kayla L. McClurg/p. 4*
This poem suggests that subjects for poetry are to be found anywhere and everywhere. Follow the advice offered in the last verse of the poem: "Look at your world,/ at what others do not see./ Wrap it in words,/ and you will have a poem." Write two more verses that illustrate the point that poetry is everywhere. You may choose to imitate the style of the poem if you wish.

Reading Poetry/*Mary McIver/p. 7*
Write a poem using the same form and style as this one. Instead of "reading poetry," have your poem focus on another activity, such as driving cars, skiing powder snow, reading novels, partying with friends, or any other topic you prefer. Try to create at least five verses for your poem.

Listen, Real Poetry Doesn't Say Anything/*Jim Morrison/p. 10*
Select one of the statements that Morrison makes, and enlarge on it. Do you agree or disagree with what he says? Why? How does the statement influence your perspective of poetry in general? Find as many examples as you can of particular poems that support your point of view.

Tentative Definitions of Poetry/*Carl Sandburg/p. 11*
Write an eleventh definition of poetry. Try to adopt the same tone and style as Sandburg, using images based on your own experiences. Illustrate your definition with original art work or with appropriate pictures from magazines.

THE GREATER PERSPECTIVE

1. What do *you* really think about poets and poetry? Write a poem either about poets or about the power of poetry. Tape record your poem, with appropriate background music. You might wish to enlist the aid of a fellow student in making your tape.

2. Working on your own, or with a few other students, prepare a dramatic reading of one or more of the poems in this unit. Share your interpretation with the class.

3. There are published poets living in many communities. Often, they are more than willing to be interviewed or to visit a classroom to talk about their work. Arrange for a local poet to visit your class. With the poet's permission, make a videotape of the visit, and place this in the school resource centre for other classes to share.

4. Research the life and achievements of one of the poets in this unit. Imagine that you have been asked to ''introduce'' this poet as a guest speaker for your school's ''Poetry Day.'' Your introduction should be under three minutes. Assume that your classmates know absolutely nothing about the poet. Be informative and concise.

2 WHEN UNICORNS WERE STILL POSSIBLE

When I was young, it seemed that life was so wonderful,
a miracle, oh it was beautiful, magical.
And all the birds in the trees, well they'd be singing so happily,
joyfully, playfully, watching me.

from The Logical Song

RICK DAVIES AND ROGER HODGSON

18

YOUTH AND AGE

Children, teenagers, and adults look out at the same world and yet see quite different things. The child's eye sees a world full of magic, wonder, and beauty. This vision is fuelled by curiosity and boundless energy. As teenagers and adults, we wonder about what happens to the child's inquisitive nature, and we mourn the loss of this special way of seeing.

Is it not significant that we often respond with admiration, envy and wistful nostalgia to the naïve wisdom of the child's perspective?

The poems in this chapter invite you to see the world as perhaps you once did, and might again—with the right perspective.

There are three ways to get something done: do it yourself, hire someone, or forbid your kids to do it.
MONTA CRANE

Children today are tyrants. They contradict their parents, gobble their food, and tyrannize their teachers.
SOCRATES (470–399 BC)

Adults are obsolete children.
DR. SEUSS

Youth is a disease from which we all recover.
DOROTHY FULDHEIM

Youth is not a time of life—it is a state of mind. It is not a matter of red cheeks, red lips, and supple knees. It is a temper of the will; a quality of the imagination; a vigour of the emotions; it is a freshness of the deep springs of life.
SAMUEL ULLMAN

CRABBED AGE AND YOUTH

WILLIAM SHAKESPEARE

Crabbed Age and Youth
Cannot live together:
Youth is full of pleasance,
Age is full of care;
Youth like summer morn,
Age like winter weather;
Youth like summer brave;
Age like winter bare.
Youth is full of sport,
Age's breath is short;
Youth is nimble, Age is lame;
Youth is hot and bold,
Age is weak and cold;
Youth is wild, and Age is tame.
Age, I do abhor thee;
Youth, I do adore thee;
O my Love, my Love is young!
Age, I do defy thee . . .

THE PHILOSOPHERS

R.G. EVERSON

```
          ladders
         park    then
        play
       high            slide
      climb
     slowly                 laughing
    they
   while                            down
  nervously
 wave                                    swift
Children                                     years
```

ALEX

PHYLLIS WEBB

at five o'clock today Alex four years old said
I will draw a picture of you!
at first he gave me no ears and I said
you should give me ears
I would like big ears one on each side
and he added them and three buttons down the front
now I'll make your skirt wide he said and he did
and he put pins in all up and down my ribs and I waited
and he said now I'll put a knife in you
it was in my side and I said does it hurt
and No! he said and we laughed and he said
now I'll put a fire on you and he put male
fire on me in the right place then scribbled me
all into flames shouting FIRE FIRE FIRE
FIRE FIRE FIRE and I said
shall we call the fire engines and he said Yes!
this is where they are and the ladders are bending
and we made siren noises and he drew the engines on
over the page then he said the Hose! and he put
the fire out and that's better I said
and he rolled over laughing like crazy
because it was all on paper

from AUGURIES OF INNOCENCE

WILLIAM BLAKE

To see a World in a Grain of Sand
And a Heaven in a Wild Flower,
Hold Infinity in the palm of your hand
And Eternity in an hour.

June Bug

PAT JASPER

This morning as I was fixing lunch,
he tore through the screen door
looking for just-the-right-size box.
He had caught a frog in our window-well
and wanted to make a home for it.

I remembered June mornings
when I was eight in Oklahoma,
catching lizards, baby birds,
nesting them in just-the-right-size box,
adding rocks for boulders
twigs for trees
peanut-butter lids of water for ponds.
We tied strings around the legs of June bugs,
tethering them like buzzy green balloons.
In the evenings we would play
swinging statues until it got dark,
then catch fireflies,
shutting them up in mayonnaise jars
where they lit up pretend lanterns.

A peculiar penchant of eight-year-olds,
capturing creatures,
holding them close in sweaty palms,
stroking their bellies until they fall asleep.
To stop life long enough to touch it.
To keep it from escaping.

Does he clamp memories into boxes too?
Screw them inside jars,
sometimes forgetting to punch holes in the top
to let them breathe?

As I watch him through the curtains,
swatting flies to feed his frog,
I want to tie a string around his leg
and keep him eight forever.

STEFAN

P.K. PAGE

Stefan
aged eleven
looked at the baby and said
When he thinks it must be pure thought
because he hasn't any words yet
and we
proud parents
admiring friends
who had looked at the baby

looked at the baby again

One of the most obvious facts about grownups to a child,
is that they have forgotten what it is like to be a child.
RANDALL JARRELL (from *The Third Book of Criticism*)

"WHAT WILL YOU BE?"

DENNIS LEE

They never stop asking me,
''What will you be?—
A doctor, a dancer,
A diver at sea?''

They never stop bugging me:
''What will you *be*?''
As if they expect me to
Stop being me.

When I grow up I'm going to be a Sneeze.
And sprinkle Germs on all my Enemies.

When I grow up I'm going to be a Toad.
And dump on Silly Questions in the road.

When I grow up, I'm going to be a Child.
I'll Play the whole darn day and drive them Wild.

OCTOPUS'S GARDEN

RINGO STARR

I'd like to be under the sea
In an octopus's garden in the shade.
He'd let us in, knows where we've been,
In his octopus's garden in the shade.
I'd ask my friends to come and see
An octopus's garden with me.

I'd like to be under the sea
In an octopus's garden in the shade.
We would be warm below the storm
In our little hideaway beneath the waves.
Resting our heads on the sea bed,
In an octopus's garden near a cave
We would sing and dance around
Because we know we can't be found.

I'd like to be under the sea
In an octopus's garden in the shade.
We would shout and swim about
The coral that lies beneath the waves,
Oh what a joy for every girl and boy
Knowing they're happy and they're safe.
We would be so happy, you and me,
No one there to tell us what to do.

I'd like to be under the sea
In an octopus's garden with you.
In an octopus's garden with you.
In an octopus's garden with you.

from ODE: INTIMATIONS OF IMMORTALITY FROM RECOLLECTIONS OF EARLY CHILDHOOD

WILLIAM WORDSWORTH

1

There was a time when meadow, grove, and stream,
The earth, and every common sight,
To me did seem
Apparelled in celestial light,
The glory and the freshness of a dream.
It is not now as it hath been of yore;—
Turn wheresoe'er I may,
By night or day,
The things which I have seen I now can see no more.

2

The Rainbow comes and goes,
And lovely is the Rose,
The Moon doth with delight
Look round her when the heavens are bare;
Waters on a starry night
Are beautiful and fair;
The sunshine is a glorious birth;
But yet I know, where'er I go,
That there hath past away a glory from the earth.

YOU'RE GROUNDED!

LIDIA TREMBLAY

200 paper airplanes
have landed on my
        bedroom floor
200 paper airplanes
I made in an
        attempt to soar

beyond the confines
of the sleepless night

Alas!

not one of them has carried me
towards the place where light
from dark is only seen
as negatives of photographs

200 paper airplanes
like gentle ghosts
        so pale
could only
        call
to me with
        rustling laughs

As

they spun around
between the walls
they touched the ceiling
        and the door

Then

200 paper airplanes
crash-landed on my
        bedroom floor

JUSTICE

LEONA GOM

I always had this craving for salt
but my mother had this horror
about my getting high blood pressure
or something so she'd put
all the salt shakers up too high
for me to reach
but I outsmarted her
for a while at least
by squatting out in the pasture
for hours at a time
and licking blissfully
the big red salt block
that a cow would usually share
with me on the other side
but mother caught me at it one day
and she paddled my bottom
right there in front of the cow
who watched in placid amusement
so I really grew to hate cows
who could lick all the salt they wanted
and never get a licking
but of course I'm old enough now
to see it's wrong to hate
those poor dumb animals
so I really pity them instead
because they'll all probably die
of high blood pressure.

A BACKWARDS JOURNEY

P.K. PAGE

When I was a child of say, seven,
I still had serious attention to give
to everyday objects. The Dutch Cleanser—
which was the kind my mother bought—
in those days came in a round container
of yellow cardboard around which ran
the very busy Dutch Cleanser woman
her face hidden behind her bonnet
holding a yellow Dutch Cleanser can
on which a smaller Dutch Cleanser woman
was holding a smaller Dutch Cleanser can
on which a minute Dutch Cleanser woman
held an imagined Dutch Cleanser can . . .

This was no game. The woman led me
backwards through the eye of the mind
until she was the smallest point
my thought could hold to. And at that moment
I think I knew that if no one called
and nothing broke the delicate jet
of my attention, that tiny image
could smash the atom of space and time.

A COFFIN AND A CHEVY

CARL LEGGO

My father bought the '53 Chevy
(maroon and new), drove my brother and me
out of the city along the Trans Canada Highway
to cut a Christmas tree, parked on the shoulder,
left my brother and me, sank into the snow
like quicksand (my brother, only four, laughing)
before he was swallowed by the trees like darkness
And I was laughing at my brother laughing
and my father waved a hand, his mouth a tight line
and my brother jumped up and down in the back seat
while I pretended to drive away (for help)
but went nowhere and my father didn't come back,
my brother full of fear, no longer laughing,
and the air was thick with chewy toffee,
my father gone, my brother going crazy,
so I grabbed the ice scraper and jabbed holes
in the maroon velvet over me like the inside
of a coffin, no escape, and my father returned,
creature from the snow lagoon, bearing a tree,
a wide grin where the line had been,
and the car was a car, not a coffin,
my father was alive, my brother was laughing,
and my father looked at the neat triangular flags
hanging from the ceiling of his new Chevy,
said nothing, drove back to the city
in a Chevy once more a coffin.

I KNOW

CAROLYN MAMCHUR

I know when my dad's
been sneaking a smoke
in the tool shed:
sweet pipe tobacco smells
stay in his hair
on his rough tweed jacket.

I know when my dad's
waking up before the alarm
goes off at seven a.m.:
his snoring stops and
starts, he breathes
out low and long and lazy.

I know when my dad's
been working too hard
under somebody else's deadline:
all the Mennen in the world
doesn't keep that
scared sour smell away.

I know when my dad's
been eating oranges
in front of the T.V.:
the juice jumps to his chin,
clings to his t-shirt
as he slices through the peel.

I know when he's been
riding in the park
through the hyacinths
by the sea wall
past the steel mill.
He brings the stories
in his hair
on his clothes
before he tells me.
And he always
tells me.

I know too,
when he's been crying;
remembering
the day he was
cooking burgers
and the barbecue
exploded
in my face.

After that
I learned to smell.
And listen.

It ain't so bad.

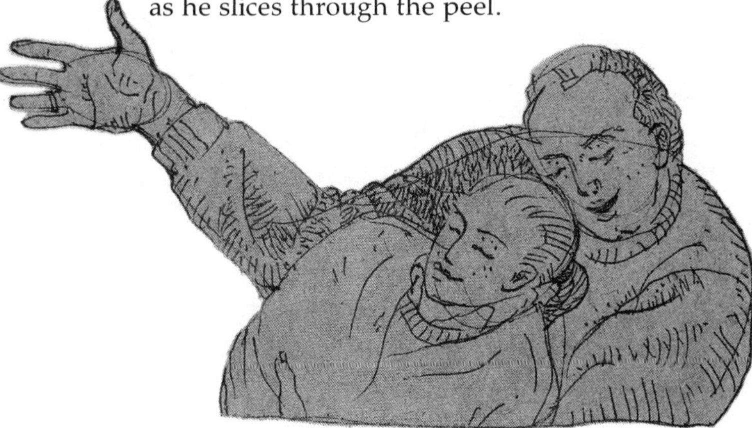

from THIS ONE'S ON ME

PHYLLIS GOTLIEB

my father managed a theatre

which one day (childhood reminiscence indicated) passing
on a Sunday ride, we found
the burglar alarm was ring
alingaling
out jumped my father and ran for the front door
Uncle Louie ran for the back
siren scream down the cartrack Danforth
and churchbells ding dong ding
(ting a ling)
and brakescreech whooee
six fat squadcars filled with the finest
of the force of our fair city
brass button boot refulgent
and in their plainclothes too
greysuit felt hat and flat black footed
and arrested Uncle Louie

Oh what a brannigan
what a brouhaha
while Mother and Aunt Gittel and me
sat in the car and shivered
delicious
ly

because a mouse bit through a wire.

THE BIG YEARS

JO LENA

I don't want
to be
a teenager
any more.

For a long time
I couldn't wait.

I'm ten
and being a
teenager was
a big deal.

Fast cars
late night T.V.
spending money
my own room
big kid places.

But yesterday
that all stopped.

Four teenagers
killed my dog.

He was on a sidewalk,
my dog, Pal, was on the
sidewalk.

Four teenagers
in a car
drove up
over the curb

to hit him.

They were laughing.
I saw them
in a red car,
four teenagers.

I buried Pal
out in the ferns
behind the creek
where ten-year-olds
and their dogs
go to play.

Teenagers never
go near the place.

THROUGH A GLASS EYE, LIGHTLY

CAROLYN KIZER

In the laboratory waiting room
containing
one television actor with a teary face
trying a contact lens;
two muscular victims of industrial accidents;
several vain women—I was one of them—
came Deborah, four, to pick up her glass eye.

It was a long day:
Deborah waiting for the blood-vessels
painted
on her iris to dry.
Her mother said that, holding Deborah
when she was born,
"First I inspected her, from toes to navel,
then stopped at her head. . . ."
We wondered why
the inspection hadn't gone the other way.
"Looking into her eye
was like looking into a volcano:

"Her vacant pupil
went whirling down, down to the foundation
of the world . . .
When she was three months old they took it out.
She giggled when she went under
the anaesthetic.
Forty-five minutes later she came back
happy! . . .

"The gas wore off, she found the hole in her face
(you know, it never bled?),
stayed happy, even when I went to pieces.
She's five, in June.

"Deborah, you get right down
from there, or I'll have to slap!"
Laughing, Deborah climbed into the lap
of one vain lady, who
had been discontented with her own beauty.
Now she held on to Deborah, looked her steadily
in the empty eye.

▲

When I was a child, I spake as a child,
I understood as a child, I thought as a child:
But when I became a man, I put away childish things.
For now we see through a glass, darkly;
ST. PAUL (I CORINTHIANS 13:11-13)

EVERY MORNING

LAURIE REID

every morning
          I watch
as the sunlight
peeks so timidly
through the clouds
and I too,
like a sunbeam,
          peer
through the clouds
of growing up
for I'm still
          a child
searching
for the elusive dream
and I have
          all
a child's power
of knowing
          I'll find it.

THE KEY OF THE KINGDOM

ED REED

When we were children
We possessed the key to a kingdom
Such as this world has yet to see.
Wherever we went;
By lakes,
Pools
And streams,
In woods,
Meadows,
And fields,
There was a world beyond belief
In which anything could be something else.
A world
Whose every corner
Would yield some new adventure or surprise.
A world
In which we ruled
And was ours alone.

Only we children had the key,
The key of the kingdom.

A world inhabited by goblins, ghosts and ghouls,
Dragons, trolls, witches, sorcerers,
Knights, fair damsels, wicked kings
And green-skinned, three-eyed floops.
A world of enchanted geography—
Magic Forests,
Glass mountains
And fountains of youth.

In this world
We held our castles
Made of T.V. boxes
Against marauding bands of Vikings
Armed with swords made of lattice
And shields taken from the tops of garbage cans.
We sailed with Columbus
Across the unchartered waters of a lily pond.
We descended.

With Captain Nemo
To 20,000 leagues beneath the bathwater.
We went west with the pioneers
By coaster wagon,
And to the East with Marco Polo
By tricycle.
We defied savage Indians
From the next block
And returned alive
In time for an afternoon nap.
We hunted fierce man-eating squirrels.
We dared damnation
By taking the trainer wheels
Off our first bicycle.
We did a zillion billion other brave.
Courageous.
Bold.
Fun things.

Now that we are older.
Wiser
And more mature
This kingdom no longer has our allegiance.
We have lost the key
And it has perished with the rust of misuse
And neglect.

Age is the grave yard
Of all our youthful hopes.
Dreams
And experiences.

Reflections on a Gift of Watermelon Pickle

JOHN TOBIAS

During that summer
When unicorns were still possible;
When the purpose of knees
Was to be skinned;
When shiny horse chestnuts
  (Hollowed out
  Fitted with straws
  Crammed with tobacco
  Stolen from butts
  in family ashtrays)
Were puffed in green lizard silence
While straddling thick branches
Far above and away
From the softening effects
Of civilization;

During that summer—
Which may never have been at all;
But which has become more real
Than the one that was—
Watermelons ruled.

Thick pink imperial slices
Melting frigidly on sun-parched tongues
Dribbling from chins;
Leaving the best part,
The black bullet seeds,
To be spit out in rapid fire
Against the wall
Against the wind
Against each other;

And when the ammunition was spent
There was always another bite:
It was a summer of limitless bites,
Of hungers quickly felt
And quickly forgotten
With the next careless gorging.

The bites are fewer now.
Each one is savoured lingeringly,
Swallowed reluctantly.

But in a jar put up by Felicity,
The summer which maybe never was
Has been captured and preserved.
And when we unscrew the lid
And slice off a piece
And let it linger on our tongue:
Unicorns become possible again.

TO YOUTH

JOHN WEAVER

This I say to you:
Be arrogant! Be true!
True to April's lust that sings
Through your veins. These sharp Springs
Matter most . . . After years
Will be time enough to sleep . . .
Carefulness . . . and tears . . .

Now while life is raw and new,
Drink it clear, drink it deep!
Let the moonlight's lunacy
Tear away your cautions.
Be proud, and mad, and young, and free!
Grasp a comet! Kick at stars
Laughingly! Fight! Dare!

Never fear, Age will catch you,
Slow you down, ere it dispatch you
To your long and solemn quiet . . .
What will matter then the riot
Of the lilacs in the wind?
What will mean—then—the crush
Of lips at hours when birds hush?
Purple, green and flame will end
In a calm, gray blend.

ADVICE TO THE YOUNG

MIRIAM WADDINGTON

1
Keep bees and
grow asparagus,
watch the tides
and listen to the
wind instead of
the politicians
make up your own
stories and believe
them if you want to
live the good life.

2
All rituals
are instincts
never fully
trust them but
study to im-
prove biology
with reason.

3
Digging trenches
for asparagus
is good for the
muscles and
waiting for the
plants to settle
teaches patience
to those who are
usually in too
much of a hurry.

4
There is morality
in bee-keeping
it teaches how
not to be afraid
of the bee swarm
it teaches how
not to be afraid of
finding new places
and building in them
all over again.

I SHOULD HAVE CAUGHT MY UNICORN WHEN I WAS

DARIA WITT

i should have caught my unicorn when i was
sixteen
because to catch a unicorn you have to
trust
and believe
and love
all with an astonishing measure of innocence.
they're crafty beasts, unicorns,
with thin legs and thick manes
and some people say
their horns are gold.
i've lost my chance to catch my unicorn
now
I'm too old
and too
caught
myself.

COMPLAINING DAY

MARY NEVILLE

I was complaining
Today.
I thought of all the
Bad Things:
    Make my bed.
    Carry out garbage.
    Go to bed earlier than
    Other kids.
    Can't watch T.V. on
    School nights.

But I remembered some
Good Things:
    Woody,
    Mother and Dad,
    Not sick much.
    Not dead,
    My bike,
    Saturday.

That is quite a
Lot
Of good ones.

FERN HILL

DYLAN THOMAS

Now as I was young and easy under the apple boughs
About the lilting house and happy as the grass was green,
  The night above the dingle starry,
    Time let me hail and climb
  Golden in the heydays of his eyes,
And honoured among wagons I was prince of the apple towns
And once below a time I lordly had the trees and leaves
    Trail with daisies and barley
  Down the rivers of the windfall light.

And as I was green and carefree, famous among the barns
About the happy yard and singing as the farm was home,
  In the sun that is young once only,
    Time let me play and be
  Golden in the mercy of his means,
And green and golden I was huntsman and herdsman, the calves
Sang to my horn, the foxes on the hills barked clear and cold,
    And the sabbath rang slowly
  In the pebbles of the holy streams.

All the sun long it was running, it was lovely, the hay—
Fields high as the house, the tunes from the chimneys, it was air
  And playing, lovely and watery
    And fire green as grass.
  And nightly under the simple stars
As I rode to sleep the owls were bearing the farm away,
All the moon long I heard, blessed among stables, the night jars
  Flying with the ricks, and horses
    Flashing into the dark.

And then to awake, and the farm, like a wanderer white
With the dew, come back, the cock on his shoulder: it was all
  Shining, it was Adam and maiden,
    The sky gathered again
  And the sun grew round that very day.
So it must have been after the birth of the simple light
In the first, spinning place, the spellbound horses walking warm
  Out of the whinnying green stable
    On to the fields of praise.

And honoured among foxes and pheasants by the gay house
Under the new-made clouds and happy as the heart was long,
  In the sun born over and over,
    I ran my heedless ways,
  My wishes raced through the house-high hay
And nothing I cared, at my sky blue trades, that time allows
In all his tuneful turning so few and such morning songs
  Before the children green and golden
    Follow him out of grace,

Nothing I cared, in the lamb white days, that time would take me
Up to the swallow-thronged loft by the shadow of my hand,
  In the moon that is always rising,
    Nor that riding to sleep
  I should hear him fly with the high fields
And wake to the farm forever fled from the childless land.
Oh as I was young and easy in the mercy of his means,
    Time held me green and dying
  Though I sang in my chains like the sea.

THE CHILD'S SIGHT

HY SOBILOFF

The child's wisdom is in saying
They say what they see when they see it
I am beginning to remember how
When I don't say it when I see it
I remember it differently

I am walking with the children
They have included me
None of us eavesdrops any more
We speak the same celestial gibberish
Our spirit ticks the same time
I feel again and am part of the inside world

The child is a little inspector when it crawls
It touches and tastes the earth
Rolls and stumbles toward the object
Zigzags like a sail
And outmanoeuvres the room

I am learning the child's way
I pick up wood pieces from the ground
And see shapes into them
I notice a purple velvet bee resting on a flower
And stop to listen to its buzz

They have included me
And though I will not be put away to rock alone
And I don't roll down the plush hills
Nor spit for luck
I am learning their way
They have given me back the bliss of my senses

Crabbed Age and Youth/*William Shakespeare*/*p. 19*
This selection appeared almost 400 years ago in a collection of poems attributed to Shakespeare entitled, "The Passionate Pilgrim." In this particular poem, the speaker expresses a number of strong opinions on "youth" and "age."

Rewrite the poem using the less formal language of today. Make sure that the contrast between the two ages is fully developed.

The Philosophers/*R.G. Everson*/*p. 19*
Writing concrete poetry is easy and fun!

Begin by choosing a familiar object that is usually associated with childhood (e.g., a baby carriage, building blocks, a baby's bottle). Then draw the shape of the object (in pencil), and fill it with related words and phrases. Use hyphens or creative spellings to make the words fit the shape if you wish. Exercise your poetic licence.

Experiment! You may need to go through a number of drafts to arrive at your final product. When you are satisfied with your poem, erase the pencilled outline.

The Big Years/*Jo Lena*/*p. 31*
Write the dialogue that might take place in one of the following situations:

a) You are a parent of the ten-year-old in the poem. You and the child discuss the incident and the child's wish never to become a teenager.
b) You were one of the four teenagers in the car. You do not approve of what the driver did, and the two of you are discussing the situation.
c) You are the ten-year-old whose dog was killed. Six years have passed since the incident. One day in a coffee shop, you overhear a conversation during which someone boasts about running over a dog on a sidewalk a few years back. You approach the table and share your thoughts and feelings on the matter.

Complaining Day/*Mary Neville*/*p. 39*
The speaker in this poem has a lot of "bad things" and "good things" in her life.

Write an entry in your journal or a letter to yourself, outlining all the things in your life that you have to complain about and be happy for.

The Child's Sight/*Hy Sobiloff*/*p. 42*
Imagine that you are related to the speaker in this poem. You have noted that his/her behaviour is not typical of people that age. Write a letter to another family member describing the speaker's activities and your reaction to them. Make some recommendations. You may, of course, choose to approve or disapprove of the behaviour.

THE GREATER PERSPECTIVE

1. Conduct an opinion poll. Prepare a list of questions that deal with the different attitudes we have towards youth and age. Phrase your items so that the same questions can be asked of both age groups.

   Interview as many people as you can. You might wish to tape-record or video-tape the interviews, with the respondent's permission.

2. Create a collage that illustrates what you consider to be the important characteristics of ''Youth and Adulthood.''

3. In groups, select one or more issues dealt with by the poems in this chapter and prepare a Readers' Theatre script that explores the group's perspective on the topic. You might choose to base your script on poems and quotations from this chapter or you might also wish to use material from other sources. Share your script with the class.

CHAPTER THREE

3 ON THE WAY TO SCHOOL

On the way to school
One morning long ago
I stopped to look at the sunrise . . .

RON SEDOR

STUDENTS AND TEACHERS

Teachers and students have their own special way of looking at the world and at each other. Frequently, these views may differ to say the least.

The feelings and issues dealt with in this chapter should be familiar to anyone who has ever set foot in a classroom. How do students and teachers see themselves and each other? What are the advantages and disadvantages of being a student and of being a teacher?

If every day in the life of a school could be the last day but one, there would be little fault to find with it.
STEPHEN LEACOCK

Education is what survives when what has been learnt has been forgotten.
B.F. SKINNER

He teaches who gives and he learns who receives.
RALPH WALDO EMERSON

What we have to learn to do, we learn by doing.
ARISTOTLE

For every person wishing to teach, there are thirty not wanting to be taught.
W.C. SELLAR

THE SCHOOLBOY

WILLIAM BLAKE

I love to rise in a summer morn
When the birds sing on every tree;
The distant huntsman winds his horn,
And the sky-lark sings with me.
O! what sweet company.

But to go to school in a summer morn,
O! it drives all joy away;
Under a cruel eye outworn,
The little ones spend the day
In sighing and dismay.

Ah! then at times I drooping sit,
And spend many an anxious hour,
Nor in my book can I take delight,
Nor sit in learning's bower,
Worn thro' with the dreary shower.

How can the bird that is born for joy
Sit in a cage and sing?
How can a child, when fears annoy,
But droop his tender wing,
And forget his youthful spring?

O! father and mother, if buds are nip'd
And blossoms blown away,
And if the tender plants are strip'd
Of their joy in the springing day,
By sorrow and care's dismay.

How shall the summer arise in joy,
Or the summer fruits appear?
Or how shall we gather what griefs destroy,
Or bless the mellowing year,
When the blasts of winter appear?

MEMORY FROM CHILDHOOD

ANTONIO MACHADO
(translated by Robert Bly)

A chilly and overcast afternoon
in winter. The students
are studying. Steady boredom
of raindrops across the windowpanes.

It is time for class. In a poster
Cain is shown running
away, and Abel dead,
not far from a red spot.

The teacher, with a voice husky and hollow,
is thundering. He is an old man badly dressed,
withered and dried up,
who is holding a book in his hand.

And the whole children's choir
is singing its lesson:
one thousand times one hundred is one hundred thousand,
one thousand times one thousand is one million.

A chilly and overcast afternoon
in winter. The students
are studying. Steady boredom
of raindrops across the windowpanes.

STUDENTS

TOM WAYMAN

The freshman class-list printouts
showed birthdates so recent
Wayman was sure the computer was in error.
One young man, however, was curious
about Wayman's mention near the start of term
of his old college newspaper:
"You were an editor *when*? Wow,
that's the year I was born."

The wisdom of the students
hadn't altered, though.
Wayman observed many clung to
The Vaccination Theory of Education
he remembered: once you have had a subject
you are immune
and never have to consider it again.
Other students continued to endorse
The Dipstick Theory of Education:
as with a car engine, where as long as the oil level
is above the add line
there is no need to put in more oil,
so if you receive a pass or higher
why put any more into learning?

At the front of the room, Wayman sweated
to reveal his alternative.
''Adopt The Kung Fu Theory of Education,''
he begged.
''Learning as self-defence. The more you understand
about what's occurring around you
the better prepared you are to deal with difficulties.''

The students remained skeptical.
A young woman was a pioneer
of The Easy Listening Theory of Learning:
spending her hours in class
with her tape recorder earphones on,
silently enjoying a pleasanter world.
''Don't worry, I can hear you,''
she reassured Wayman
when after some days he was moved to inquire.

Finally, at term's end
Wayman inscribed after each now-familiar name on the list
the traditional single letter.
And whatever pedagogical approach
he or the students espoused,
Wayman knew this notation would be pored over
with more intensity
than anything else Wayman taught.

COMPUTER REPORT CARD

MEGUIDO ZOLA

l a x a t t e n d a n c e
e f f o r t s n e e d e d
n o t s o p u n c t u a l
j u s t n o t t r y i n g
p o o r b e h a v i o u r
m u s t g e t w i t h i t
r e a d i n g p o o r l y
c o u l d d o b e t t e r
s p e l l s s o b a d l y
c a n i m p r o v e n o w
w r i t i n g s l o p p y
m u s t g e t t i d i e r
g a p s i n g r a m m a r
k e e p o n w o r k i n g
m a t h ' s n o t e a s y
s l o w i n s o c i a l s
k e e p u p p a c e n o w
a r t i s s l i p p i n g
n o i m p r o v e m e n t
g y m ' s a p r o b l e m
c a n d o m u c h m o r e
w e a k i n b a s i c s !
p o o r a c h i e v e r !
f i n a l w a r n i n g !

DISILLUSIONMENT

GAYLE REYNOLDS

In my classroom today
A boy slept
And upon awakening
Engraved
In the formica of his desktop
That word
Which makes me shudder.

And I
Had tried so hard,
Bouncing about the room
(Though my legs ached),
Causing my voice to rise
And fall
To avoid a monotone,
Laughing easily
(Though my uncle's death was heavy on me),
Speaking words and phrases I had prepared
To be effective.

And when the bell
Rang
Those eager to be free
And those eager to be first
Raced
From my room
Plunging into the mass
In the hall.

Others,
More patient, but relieved,
Flowed out the open door on
The heels of their fellows.

The lingerers,
Needing still more attention,
Requiring still more notice
From someone,
Paused by my desk.

And then I was alone
With that word on the desk,
With a dictionary someone had avoided putting
  away
By sliding it under his desk,
And with my disillusionment.

OCCUPATION

PAT SARGENT

I teach,
Words are my business.
I fling them against the firmament
And watch them fall as shooting stars.
Someday one may stick
And shed its soft light forever.

▲

The entire object of true education
is to make people not merely do the right thing
but enjoy the right thing.
JOHN RUSKIN

TEACHERS

MICHAEL ROSEN

Rodge said,
''Teachers—they want it all ways—
You're jumping up and down on a chair
or something
and they grab hold of you and say,
'Would you do that sort of thing in your own
home?'

So you say, 'No.'
And they say,
'Well, don't do it here then.'

But if you say, 'Yes, I do it at home.'
they say,
'Well we don't want that sort of thing
going on here
thank you very much.'

Teachers—they get you all ways,''
Rodge said.

PTERODACTYLS

MARJORIE L. SALLEE

Never trust a teacher with tantalizing eyes
Or pterodactyls on his tie,
Who collects strange toys
And bids on junk at auctions.
He will pull you into poetry
And hook your mind on literary history.
Then, when you need to tune him out,
You can't. And years later
His voice still haunts you
Sending you in search of
Books you haven't read yet.

Those pterodactyls might have warned
Of the persistence of his instruction.
Their species may have vanished,
But like the poets in the book
He made them breathe again for us.

▲

It is the supreme art of the teacher
to awaken joy in creative expression and knowledge.
ALBERT EINSTEIN

EDUCATOR

SHELLY BARGE

I look up to you
only because I'm short.
You anger me
with your ancient ways.
You push my creativity
and pull what you need.

Pompous authority
has gone to your head.
You may be correct
and I might be crazy,
but your world
will come unsewn,
and I will hold the only needle.

THE ROBINS SANG AND SANG AND SANG

ALBERT CULLUM

The robins sang and sang and sang,
but teacher you went right on.
The last bell sounded the end of the day,
but teacher you went right on.
The geranium on the window sill just died,
but teacher you went right on.

THE NATURE LESSON

MARJORIE BALDWIN

The teacher has the flowers on her desk,
Then goes round, giving one to each of us.
We are going to study the primrose—
To find out all about it. It has five petals,
(Notice the little dent in each, making it heart-shaped)
And a pale green calyx (and O! the hairy stem!)
Now, in the middle of the flower
There may be a little knob—that is the pistil—
Or perhaps your flower may show the bunch of stamens.
        We look at our flowers
To find out which kind we have got.

Now we are going to look inside,
So pull your petals off, one by one.
        But wait . . .
If I pull my flower to pieces it will stop
Being a primrose. It will be just bits
Strewn on my desk. I can't pull it to pieces.
What does it matter what goes on inside?
I won't find out by pulling it to pieces,
Because it will not be a primrose any more,
And the bits will not mean anything at all.
A primrose is a primrose, not just bits.

It lies there, five-petalled primrose—
A whole primrose, a living primrose.
To find out what is inside I make it dead,
And then it will not be a primrose.

You can't find out
What goes on inside a living flower that way.
The teacher talks, fingers rustle . . .
I will look over my neighbour's flower
And leave my primrose whole. But if the teacher comes
And tells me singly to pull my flower to pieces
Then I will do as I am told. The teacher comes,
Passes my neighbour on her gangway side,
Does not see my primrose is still whole,

Goes by, not noticing; nobody notices.
My flower remains a primrose, that they all
Want to find out about by pulling to pieces.
I am alone: all the world is alone
In the flower left breathing on my desk.

ON THE WAY TO SCHOOL

RON SEDOR

On the way to school
One morning long ago
I stopped to look
At the sunrise
I looked too long
I missed my bus
I failed school
I got a crumby job
I spent my life
Looking at sunrises
And sunsets
I lived in poverty
And died rich.

BIRD IN THE CLASSROOM

COLIN THIELE

The students drowsed and drowned
in the teacher's ponderous monotone—
Limp bodies looping in the wordy heat,
Melted and run together, desks and flesh as one,
Swooning and swimming in a sea of drone.

Each one asleep, swayed and vaguely drifted
With lidding eyes and lolling, weighted heads,
Was caught on heavy waves and dimly lifted,
Sunk slowly, ears ringing, in the syrup of his sound,
Or borne from the room on a heaving wilderness of beds.

And then, on a sudden, a bird's cool voice
Punched out song. Crisp and spare
On the startled air,
Beak-beamed
Or idly tossed,
Each note gleamed
Like a bead of frost.

A bird's cool voice from a neighbour tree
With five clear calls—mere grains of sound
Rare and neat
Repeated twice . . .
But they sprang the heat
Like drops of ice.

Ears cocked, before the comment ran
Fading and chuckling where a wattle stirred,
The students wondered how they could have heard
Such dreary monotones from man,
Such wisdom from a bird.

To David, About His Education

HOWARD NEMEROV

The world is full of mostly invisible things,
And there is no way but putting the mind's eye,
Or its nose, in a book, to find them out,
Things like the square root of Everest
Or how many times Byron goes into Texas,
Or whether the law of the excluded middle
Applies west of the Rockies. For these
And the like reasons, you have to go to school
And study books and listen to what you are told,
And sometimes try to remember. Though I don't know
What you will do with the mean annual rainfall
On Plato's Republic, or the calorie content
Of the Diet of Worms, such things are said to be
Good for you, and you will have to learn them
In order to become one of the grown-ups
Who sees invisible things neither steadily nor whole,
But keeps gravely the grand confusion of the world
Under his hat, which is where it belongs,
And teaches small children to do this in their turn.

FOREIGN STUDENT

BARBARA B. ROBINSON

In September she appeared
  row three, seat seven,
  heavy pleated skirt,
  plastic purse, tidy notepad,
there she sat,
silent,
straight from Tai Pei,
and she bowed
when I entered the room.
A model student
I noticed,
  though she walked
  alone through the halls,
every assignment neat,
on time, complete,
and she'd listen
when I talked.

But now it's May
and Si Lan
is called Lani.
She strides in
with Noriyo and Lynne
and Natavidad.
She wears slacks.
Her gear is crammed
into a macramé
shoulder sack.
And she chatters with Pete
during class
and
I'm glad.

A POEM FOR HIGH SCHOOL ANTHOLOGIES

GEORGE BOWERING

This will be serious, literature,
& Canadian, you'll have to look out for
the author's intentions, & also
his tricks, his puns, his jokes, the things
he is doing to make it
difficult
& hence worthwhile, Right?

Pay attention. You might be askt:
what is the most vivid figure of speech
in this selection? Just remember this:

The ivory wings of the white bird
fell off & woke the sleeping maiden
who gently lifted her feet
from the oven, piping hot!

Now you may ask yourself, what
does that symbolize, & as a matter of fact
why does the author say what
at the end of the line?

Oh, I forgot,
George Bowering was born in
Princeton, British Columbia,
December 1st, 1939, the son of
a high school Latin teacher.

There are various references to the student in this poem.
Why do you think the author keeps coming back
to that subject?

What do you think his attitude to the student is?
Pick out key words & phrases that
drive his point home.

Slave.
Lazy.
Longing for a cool mountainside & a filtertip smoke.
Forced to read a difficult poem.

She said I love you more than Mike Hunt.
Even more than reading a poem by a Canadian poet.
Does this poet know what he's doing?

How appropriate is the title?

LIES

YEVGENY YEVTUSHENKO

Telling lies to the young is wrong.
Proving to them that lies are true is wrong.
Telling them that God's in his heaven
and all's well with the world is wrong.
The young know what you mean. The young are people.
Tell them the difficulties can't be counted,
and let them see not only what will be
but see with clarity these present times.
Say obstacles exist they must encounter
sorrow happens, hardship happens.
The hell with it. Who never knew
the price of happiness will not be happy.
Forgive no error you recognize,
it will repeat itself, increase,
and afterwards our pupils
will not forgive in us what we forgave.

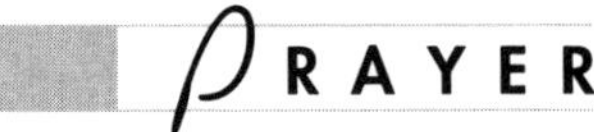

PRAYER

BP NICHOL

teach me song. i
would sing. teach me
love. i would
i were open
to it. teach me
to pray
privately, praise
quietly
those things
i should. show me
the grace
of movement
& touch—that much
i would offer
to her. teach me
more—a way
for me
to reach her
who beckons
hesitantly. teach me
to be sure.

The Schoolboy/*William Blake*/*p. 47*
Even though Blake's poem was written almost two hundred years ago, it seems that young people's attitudes towards school have changed little over the years.

Rewrite the poem as a monologue or dialogue in which a high school student attempts to convince a parent that it would be all right to miss school on this particular warm June day.

Students/*Tom Wayman*/*p. 48*
Wayman offers four different "theories of education." Based on your observations of students, teachers and classrooms, write a description of at least two other theories that you feel are "clung to" in your school.

Disillusionment/*Gayle Reynolds*/*p. 51*
Imagine you are the student who slept through the class and who wrote the word on the desk. Later that same day, you discover that your teacher is having a rough time coping with the death of her uncle. You feel terrible about your behaviour and you decide to write her a sympathy card with a note of apology. Design an appropriate sympathy card. You may use a professional store-bought card as a model if you wish. Write the note on the card.

Educator/*Shelly Barge*/*p. 53*
You are a former student of the teacher described in the poem. It is ten years after graduation and you have entered one of the service professions such as medicine, law, law enforcement, psychology, auto mechanics and income-tax auditing, to name a few. One day, much to your surprise (and pleasure because the past has not been forgotten), your ex-teacher walks into your life, in need of your help. Write a short story that describes what takes place during this reunion. Try to make the confrontation humorous rather than vindictive.

The Nature Lesson/*Marjorie Baldwin*/*p. 54*
Write a letter to the editor of your local or school newspaper outlining your views on whether or not students should be forced to perform dissections in science classes. Give reasons to support your opinion.

Lies/*Yevgeny Yevtushenko*/*p. 60*
Is it ever "right" to tell lies? Prepare a short speech that outlines your views. Present your speech to the class.

THE GREATER PERSPECTIVE

1. What are the characteristics of the "ideal" teacher, student and school? Work with a partner and survey several students or classes in your school. Prepare the results of your findings in chart form.
2. Design a magazine ad or TV commercial to promote what you consider to be an ideal classroom. You may choose to treat the subject seriously or you may wish to parody a popular ad campaign.

4 NOTHING GOLD CAN STAY

But pleasures are like poppies spread—
You seize the flow'r, its bloom is shed;
Or like the snow falls in the river—
A moment white—then melts for ever.

from Tam o'Shanter

ROBERT BURNS

CARPE DIEM

The older we get, the more aware we become of the swift passage of time. We know in our hearts that we will never be what we once were in terms of youth, energy, beauty and strength. We may even feel at times that if we do not "seize the day" and make the most of what pleasures are available to us now, we may one day regret the missed opportunities.

The carpe diem theme emphasizes the value of present, immediate joys over possible future pleasures that we cannot really count on. It is argued that since we do not know what tomorrow will bring, we should enjoy ourselves today.

Do you agree with this sentiment?

Carpe diem, quam minimum credula postero
(seize the day, do not rely on the future)
HORACE (65–8 BC)

Live all you can; it's a mistake not to. It doesn't matter so much what you do in particular, so long as you live your life. If you haven't had that, what have *you had?*
HENRY JAMES

Life is short. Live it up.
NIKITA KRUSCHEV

People do not live nowadays—they get about ten per cent out of life.
ISADORA DUNCAN

Like as the waves make to the pebbled shore,
So do our minutes hasten to their end.
WILLIAM SHAKESPEARE

The gardener's rule applies to youth and age:
When young sow wild oats, but when old, grow sage.
H. J. BYRON

NOTHING GOLD CAN STAY

ROBERT FROST

Nature's first green is gold,
Her hardest hue to hold.
Her early leaf's a flower;
But only so an hour.
Then leaf subsides to leaf.
So Eden sank to grief,
So dawn goes down to day.
Nothing gold can stay.

YOU WILL DIE

CONFUCIUS
(translated by H. A. Giles)

You have coats and robes,
But you do not trail them;
You have chariots and horses,
But you do not ride them.
By and by you will die,
And another will enjoy them.

You have courtyards and halls,
But they are not sprinkled and swept;
You have bells and drums,
But they are not struck.
By and by you will die,
And another will possess them.

You have wine and food;
Why not play daily on your lute,
That you may enjoy yourself now
And lengthen your days?
By and by you will die,
And another will take your place.

To a Fat Lady Seen from the Train

FRANCES CORNFORD

O why do you walk through the fields in gloves,
  Missing so much and so much?
O fat white woman whom nobody loves,
Why do you walk through the fields in gloves,
When the grass is soft as the breast of doves
  And shivering-sweet to the touch?
O why do you walk through the fields in gloves,
  Missing so much and so much.

To His Coy Mistress

ANDREW MARVELL

Had we but world enough, and time,
This coyness, lady, were no crime.
We would sit down, and think which way
To walk, and pass our long love's day.
Thou by the Indian Ganges' side
Shouldst rubies find: I by the tide
Of Humber would complain. I would
Love you ten years before the flood,
And you should, if you please, refuse
Till the conversion of the Jews;
My vegetable love should grow
Vaster than empires and more slow;
An hundred years should go to praise
Thine eyes, and on thy forehead gaze;
Two hundred to adore each breast,
But thirty thousand to the rest;
An age at least to every part,
And the last age should show your heart.
For, lady, you deserve this state;
Nor would I love at lower rate.

But at my back I always hear
Time's winged chariot hurrying near;
And yonder all before us lie
Deserts of vast eternity.

Thy beauty shall no more be found,
Nor in thy marble vault shall sound
My echoing song; then worms shall try
That long preserved virginity;
And your quaint honour turn to dust,
And into ashes all my lust:
The grave's a fine and private place,
But none, I think, do there embrace.

Now therefore, while the youthful hue
Sits on thy skin like morning dew,
And while thy willing soul transpires
At every pore with instant fires,
Now let us sport us while we may,
And now, like amorous birds of prey,
Rather at once our time devour
Than languish in his slow-chapped power,
Let us roll all our strength and all
Our sweetness up into one ball,
And tear our pleasures with rough strife
Thorough the iron gates of life:
Thus, though we cannot make our sun
Stand still, yet we will make him run.

A TRUE POEM

DAVID McFADDEN

Seeing, hearing & smelling said six year-old Alison
when asked what she liked best about life,
making the Philosophers look kind of silly

Gather Ye Rose-Buds

ROBERT HERRICK

Gather ye rose-buds while ye may,
  Old Time is still a-flying:
And this same flower that smiles today,
  Tomorrow will be dying.

The glorious lamp of heaven, the Sun,
  The higher he's a-getting
The sooner will his race be run,
  And nearer he's to setting.

That age is best which is the first,
  When youth and blood are warmer;
But being spent, the worse, and worst
  Times still succeed the former.

Then be not coy, but use your time,
  And while ye may, go marry;
For having lost but once your prime,
  You may for ever tarry.

Refutation

IRVING LAYTON

Why did the famous poets lie to me?
Why did they tell me that the blood runs cold?
I, a simpleton, took them at their word
Who now by your grace am so wildly stirred
I shout like a madman from ecstasy,
My temples pounding though I am grey and old.

THE DIFFERENCE

DOROTHY LIVESAY

Your way of loving is too slow for me.
For you, I think, must know a tree by heart
Four seasons through, and note each single leaf
With microscopic glance before it falls—
And after watching soberly the turn
Of autumn into winter and the slow
Awakening again, the rise of sap—
Then only will you cry: "I love this tree!"

As if the beauty of the thing could be
Made lovelier or marred by any mood
Of wind, or by the sun's caprice; as if
All beauty had not sprung up with the seed.—
With such slow ways you find no time to love
A falling flame, a flower's brevity.

THE CHALLENGE

FROM THE SANSKRIT

Listen to the exhortation of the dawn!
Look to this Day!
For it is life, the very life of life.
In its brief course lie all the verities
And realities of your existence:
The glory of action, the bliss of growth,
The splendour of beauty:

For yesterday is but a dream,
And tomorrow is only a vision;
But today, well lived, makes
Every yesterday a dream of happiness
And every tomorrow a vision of hope.
Look well, therefore, to this Day!
Such is the salutation of the Dawn.

LESTER TELLS OF WANDA AND THE BIG SNOW

PAUL ZIMMER

Some years back I worked a strip mine
Out near Tylersburg. One day it starts
To snow and by two we got three feet.
I says to the foreman, "I'm going home."
He says, "Ain't you staying till five?"
I says, "I have to see to my cows,"
Not telling how Wanda was there at the house.
By the time I make it home at four
Another foot is down and it don't quit
Until it lays another. Wanda and me
For three whole days seen no one else.
We tunneled the drifts, we slid
Right over the barbed wire and laughed
At how our heartbeats melted the snow.
After a time the food was gone and I thought
I would butcher a cow, but then it cleared
And the moon come up as sweet as an apple.
Next morning the ploughs got through. It made us sad.
It don't snow like that no more. Too bad.

from A FEW FIGS FROM THISTLES

EDNA ST. VINCENT MILLAY

My candle burns at both ends;
  It will not last the night;
But ah, my foes, and oh, my friends—
  It gives a lovely light!

SECOND DEGREE BURNS

GWENDOLYN MacEWEN

My friend at the party said:
You'll get second-degree burns
If you keep sneaking through the fire

I wasn't sneaking
I was hovering with my hand
And anyway
It wasn't fire
But a candle

A candle involves fire, but
So does a hand

Trees involve fire
Streetcars involve fire

We all have second-degree burns
And they hurt but the hurt doesn't matter

The living flame of the world is what matters
The fire is edible, and now

BLUE MAGIC

ELEANOR FARJEON

In the woods the bluebells seem
Like a blue and magic dream,
Blue water, light and air
        Flow among them there.

But the eager girl who pulls
Bluebells up in basketfuls
When she gets them home will find
        The magic left behind.

THE FROST

TZU YEH

Young man,
Seize every minute
Of your time.
The days fly by;
Ere long you too
Will grow old.

If you believe me not,
See there, in the courtyard,
How the frost
Glitters white and cold and cruel
On the grass
That once was green.

ORANGE LEAVES ARE GONE

IZUMI SHIKIBU

Orange leaves are gone,
ripped away by cold night
and winter rain.
If only yesterday we'd gone
to see the mountains!

FIRE GARDENS

GWENDOLYN MacEWEN

We sped through galaxies like burning gardens
and long-travelling light linked your eye
with mine, there in the hollow part of time.
As beams unbroken, our light years
outdistanced our dark, and many sun-flowers
burst our dreams, and there were
alien moons that orbited the heart.

Somehow the continents of night were sinking
and the huge wild gardens disappeared.
Love, we endured love as the night endured
its suns and stars, and finally far blackness
was the meaning of our light.
And O, we had meant forever to rewrite
the mathematics of a thousand worlds
and chase escaping suns
down fiery paths of night.

But a collision of love stole time and breath
in a garden whose flowers were flames
which burned beyond death.

Living Is

PIET HEIN

Living is
  a thing you do
now or never—
  which do you

Lesson of the Moth

DON MARQUIS

i was talking to a moth
the other evening
he was trying to break into
an electric light bulb
and fry himself on the wires

why do you fellows
pull this stunt i asked him
because it is the conventional
thing for moths or why
if that had been an uncovered
candle instead of an electric
light bulb you would
now be a small unsightly cinder
have you no sense

plenty of it he answered
but at times we get tired
of using it
we get bored with the routine
and crave beauty
and excitement
fire is beautiful

and we know that if we get
too close it will kill us
but what does that matter
it is better to be happy
for a moment
and be burned up with beauty
than to live a long time
and be bored all the while
so we wad all our life up
into one little roll
and then we shoot the roll
that is what life is for
it is better to be a part of beauty
for one instant and then cease to
exist than to exist forever
and never be a part of beauty
our attitude toward life
is come easy go easy
we are like human beings
used to be before they became
too civilized to enjoy themselves

and before i could argue him
out of his philosophy
he went and immolated himself
on a patent cigar lighter
i do not agree with him
myself i would rather have
half the happiness and twice
the longevity

but at the same time i wish
there was something i wanted
as badly as he wanted to fry himself

archy

THE ACT

WILLIAM CARLOS WILLIAMS

There were the roses, in the rain.
Don't cut them, I pleaded.
        They won't last, she said
But they're so beautiful
        where they are.
Agh, we were all beautiful once, she
        said,
and cut them and gave them to me
        in my hand.

BARTER

SARA TEASDALE

Life has loveliness to sell,
    All beautiful and splendid things,
Blue waves whitened on a cliff,
    Soaring fire that sways and sings,
And children's faces looking up,
Holding wonder like a cup.

Life has loveliness to sell,
    Music like a curve of gold,
Scent of pine trees in the rain,
    Eyes that love you, arms that hold,
And for your spirit's still delight,
Holy thoughts that star the night.

Spend all you have for loveliness,
    Buy it and never count the cost;
For one white singing hour of peace
    Count many a year of strife well lost,
And for a breath of ecstasy
Give all you have been, or could be.

THE LILAC POEM

RAYMOND SOUSTER

Before the lilacs are over and they are only
shrunken stalks at the ends of drooping branches,
I want to write a poem about them and their beauty
brief and star-shining as a young girl's promise.

Because there is so much made of strength and wealth
and power,
because the little things are lost in this world,
I write this poem about lilacs knowing that both
are this day's only: tomorrow they will lie forgotten.

NEW NAMES

F.R. SCOTT

Let us give new names
To the stars.
What does Venus mean
Or Mars?

The tall pines on the hill
Have seen no blood.
Beneath them no men or maids
Have woo'd.

Who would read old myths
By this lake
Where the wild duck paddle forth
At daybreak?

I am more moved by the lake sheen
When night is come
Than by all the tales of Babylon
Or Rome.

Look! The moon's path is broken
By rippling bars.
I think we should give new names
To the stars.

You Will Die/*Confucius*/*p. 65*
Confucius lived almost 2000 years ago. Bring the poem up to date by substituting more modern objects, possessions and activities. You may follow the original pattern and style of the poem as closely as you like.

Second Degree Burns/*Gwendolyn MacEwen*/*p. 71*
Imagine that one of your friends has been behaving in a very ''carpe diem'' way. Write the dialogue that might take place when you attempt to warn your friend that his or her behaviour may lead to trouble of one sort or another. Try to parallel what is said in the poem, but avoid using figurative devices. You will need to invent specific details about characters and situations to make the dialogue realistic.

New Names/*F.R. Scott*/*p. 75*
How do you feel about Scott's objection to the stars and planets being named after mythological characters and his suggestions that we come up with new names?

Write a letter to Scott, either agreeing or disagreeing with his suggestion. Be sure to include reasons for your opinion.

THE GREATER PERSPECTIVE

1. The carpe diem theme is a common one in many pop lyrics. Find one or more songs that contain lines or verses that fit this theme. Transcribe the words onto transparencies and share them with the class.

2. Magazine advertisements frequently contain words and graphics associated with the carpe diem theme. Using illustrations from such advertisements, create a collage or poster that you feel makes a statement about the carpe diem philosophy.

3. You have been invited to be guest speaker at a meeting of the local senior citizens' club. The topic they have asked you to address is ''Carpe diem.'' Prepare the speech you will give, using as many audio-visual aids for it as you can. Deliver your speech to the class.

5 A LOVER'S EYES

A lover's eyes will gaze an eagle blind,
A lover's ear will hear the lowest sound . . .
Love's feeling is more soft and sensible
Than art the tender horns of cockled snails . . .
For valour, is not Love a Hercules? . . .
And when Love speaks, the voice of all the gods
Makes heaven drowsy with the harmony.
Never durst poet touch a pen to write
Until his ink were temp'red with love's sighs.

from Love's Labour's Lost

WILLIAM SHAKESPEARE

L O V E

Shakespeare once said that love ''adds a special seeing to the eye.'' Indeed, the lover, like the poet, looks at the world through very special eyes. People change when they fall in love—as do their perspectives. The same is true when they fall out of love.

The poems in this chapter recreate the world as seen through the eyes of love gained and love lost.

Love is like the measles; we all have to go
through with it.
JEROME K. JEROME

> *I am two fools, I know,*
> *For loving, and for saying so*
> *In whining Poetry.*
> JOHN DONNE

To fear love is to fear life, and those who fear
life are already three parts dead.
BERTRAND RUSSELL

> *Love is like the rose;*
> *so sweet that one always tries to gather it*
> *in spite of the thorns.*
> AUTHOR UNKNOWN

Life is a flower of which love is the honey.
VICTOR HUGO

A BLESSING

JAMES WRIGHT

Just off the highway to Rochester, Minnesota,
Twilight bounds softly forth on the grass.
And the eyes of those two Indian ponies
Darken with kindness.
They have come gladly out of the willows
To welcome my friend and me.
We step over the barbed wire into the pasture
Where they have been grazing all day, alone.
They ripple tensely, they can hardly contain their happiness
That we have come.
They bow shyly as wet swans. They love each other.
There is no loneliness like theirs.
At home once more,
They begin munching the young tufts of spring in the darkness.
I would like to hold the slenderer one in my arms,
For she has walked over to me
And nuzzled my left hand.
She is black and white,
Her mane falls wild on her forehead,
And the light breeze moves me to caress her long ear
That is delicate as the skin over a girl's wrist.
Suddenly I realize
That if I stepped out of my body I would break
Into blossom.

LOVE POEM

ROBERT BLY

When we are in love, we love the grass,
And the barns, and the lightpoles,
And the small mainstreets abandoned all night.

Strawberries

EDWIN MORGAN

There were never strawberries
like the ones we had
that sultry afternoon
sitting on the step
of the open french window
facing each other
your knees held in mine
the blue plates in our laps
the strawberries glistening
in the hot sunlight
we dipped them in sugar
looking at each other
not hurrying the feast
for one to come
the empty plates
laid on the stone together
with the two forks crossed
and I bent towards you
sweet in that air
in my arms
abandoned like a child
from your eager mouth
the taste of strawberries
in my memory
lean back again
let me love you
let the sun beat
on our forgetfulness
one hour of all
the heat intense
and summer lightning
on the Kilpatrick hills

let the storm wash the plates

IN SPRING

LOUIS DUDEK

In spring, the air is magnetic,
wherever girls and boys meet
the eyes are north and south poles
oscillating in unison.

In spring the young are especially graceful—
six-year-olds tumble like sweet potatoes,
boys of eight get rapacious,
girls go dreamy.

And the wreck of fire-escapes seems blacker
in the shining morning;
and the black bean of the sick, shaven slum child
in the iron seems entangled.

Yet love insists on being important:
youth and sweet-sixteen lean on the doorpost
at evening—
Clark Gable and Lana Turner.

The stars melt like snowdrops.
A warm wind erases
the rising vapour of the city from view,
and even the refuse in the streets
looks romantic.

URCEUS EXIT

AUSTIN DOBSON

I intended an Ode,
  And it turned to a Sonnet.
It began *à la mode*,
I intended an Ode;
But Rose crossed the road
  In her latest bonnet;
I intended an Ode;
  And it turned to a Sonnet.

ADOLESCENCE

P.K. PAGE

In love they wore themselves in a green embrace.
A silken rain fell through the spring upon them.
In the park she fed the swans and he
whittled nervously with his strange hands
And white was mixed with all their colours
as if they drew it from the flowering trees.

At night his two-finger whistle brought her down
the waterfall stairs to his shy smile
which, like an eddy, turned her round and round
lazily and slowly so her will
was nowhere—as in dreams things are and aren't.

Walking along the avenues in the dark
street lamps sang like sopranos in their heads
with a violence they never understood
and all their movements when they were together
had no conclusion.

Only leaning into the question had they motion:
after they parted were savage and swift as gulls.
Asking and asking the hostile emptiness
they were as sharp as partly sculptured stone
and all who watched, forgetting, were amazed
to see them form and fade before their eyes.

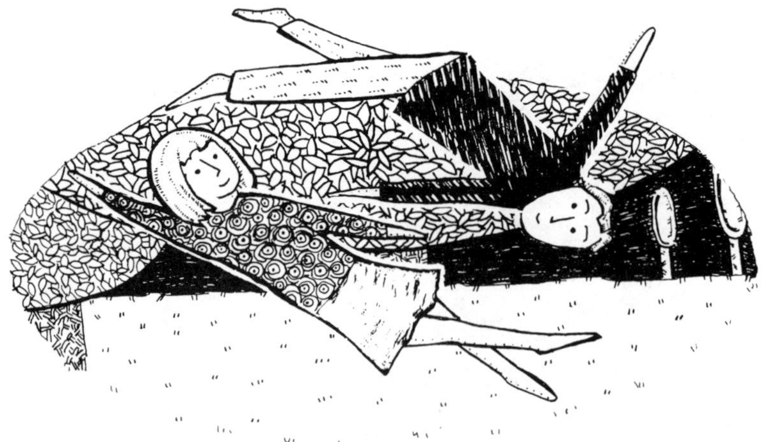

How Do I Love Thee? Let Me Count the Ways

ELIZABETH BARRETT BROWNING

How do I love thee? Let me count the ways.
I love thee to the depth and breadth and height
My soul can reach, when feeling out of sight
For the ends of Being and ideal Grace.
I love thee to the level of everyday's
Most quiet need, by sun and candle-light.
I love thee freely, as men strive for Right;
I love thee purely, as they turn from Praise.
I love thee with the passion put to use
In my old griefs, and with my childhood's faith.
I love thee with a love I seemed to lose
With my lost saints,—I love thee with the breath,
Smiles, tears, of all my life!—and, if God choose,
I shall but love thee better after death.

Shall I Compare Thee to a Summer's Day?

WILLIAM SHAKESPEARE

Shall I compare thee to a summer's day?
Thou art more lovely and more temperate:
Rough winds do shake the darling buds of May,
And summer's lease hath all too short a date:
Sometime too hot the eye of heaven shines,
And often is his gold complexion dimm'd;
And every fair from fair sometime declines,
By chance, or nature's changing course untrimm'd;
But thy eternal summer shall not fade,
Nor lose possession of that fair thou ow'st,
Nor shall death brag thou wander'st in his shade,
When in eternal lines to time thou grow'st,
  So long as men can breathe, or eyes can see,
  So long lives this, and this gives life to thee.

COMMON MAGIC

BRONWEN WALLACE

Your best friend falls in love
and her brain turns to water.
You can watch her lips move,
making the customary sounds,
but you can see they're merely
words, flimsy as bubbles rising
from some golden sea where she
swims sleek and exotic as a mermaid.

It's always like that.
You stop for lunch in a crowded
restaurant and the waitress floats
towards you. You can tell she doesn't care
whether you have the baked or French fried
and you wonder if your voice comes
in bubbles too.

It's not just women either. Or love
for that matter. The old man
across from you on the bus holds
a young child on his knee; he is singing
to her and his voice is a small boy
turning somersaults in the green
country of his blood.
It's only when the driver calls his stop
that he emerges into this puzzle
of brick and tidy hedges. Only then
you notice his shaking hands, his need
of the child to guide him home.

All over the city
you move in your own seasons
through the seasons of others: old women, faces
clawed by weather you can't feel
clack dry tongues at passersby
while adolescents seethe
in their glassy atmospheres of anger.

In parks, the children
are alien life-forms, rooted
in the galaxies they've grown through
to get here. Their games weave
the interface and their laughter
tickles that part of your brain where smells
are hidden and the nuzzling textures of things.

It's a wonder anything gets done
at all: a mechanic flails
at the muffler of your car
through whatever storm he's trapped inside
and the mailman stares at numbers
from the haze of a distant summer.

Yet somehow letters arrive and buses
remember their routes. Banks balance.
Mangoes ripen on the supermarket shelves.
Everyone manages. You gulp the thin air
of this planet as if it were the only
one you knew. Even the earth you're
standing on seems solid enough.
It's always the chance word, unthinking
gesture that unlocks the face before you.
Reveals the intricate countries
deep within the eyes. The hidden
lives, like sudden miracles,
that breathe there.

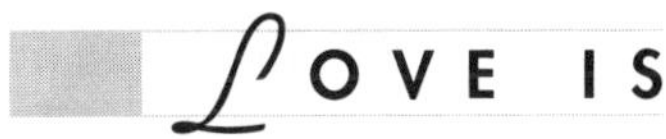

ANN DARR

a flock of birds, soaring, twisting, turning, floating, lifting, swooping, landing, splitting into pieces (individual birds) that can peck peck peck before they once again unite in the flock that, rising, goes reeling, shifting, flying (flying, that's the word I was looking for) right out of sight.

TODAY AS I PASSED THROUGH THE MARKET-PLACE

ROBERT HILLYER

Today as I passed through the market-place,
I saw so many things that you might want;
Don't scold me, I was not extravagant,—
A few necessities, that's all, in case
You should be lonely: a papyrus plant
From Egypt; an old saint with a green face;
A unicorn,—quite tame; a bit of lace
Woven from cobwebs; and an elephant.
Please don't be cross; I sold a poem today,
And really you must have these useful things;
Look! here's the best of all; I can not say
Just what it is, but it has lovely wings,
Shines like a rainbow, too. Good God! It's gone.
Kiss me. Don't cry. I'll find another one.

I SOUGHT ALL OVER THE WORLD

JOHN TAGLIABUE

I sought all over the world for a present for you until I found
the sky
And in it was the world and you and me. I was there with
my love bright as the sun
You were there with your love moony as the night, dark, and
pearls were everywhere for lovers,
The children climbed the trees on that bright and light day.
I looked all over the world
For a present for you and then I made you see yourself
and me in creation
In God and then I was, we were, very happy. The children
laughed in the tree.

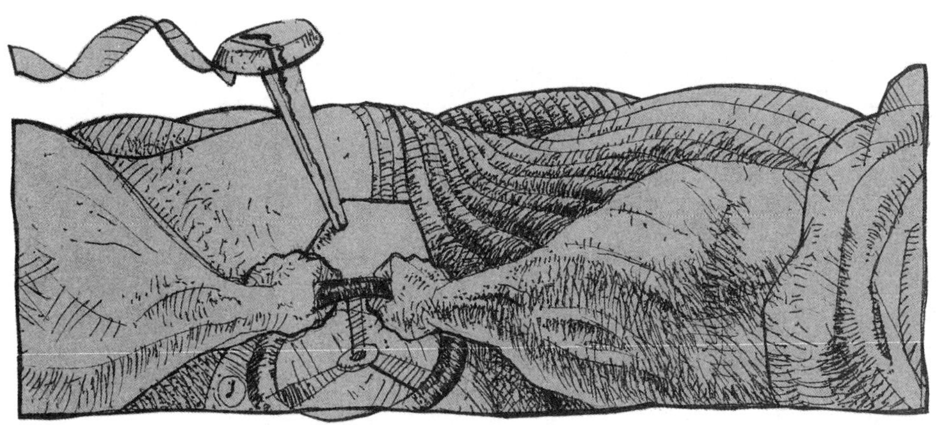

PLANTING

YVONNE TRAINER

This morning the veins swelled in my arm
purple as alfalfa flowers

If you pry my fingers open
I will show you blisters

Gripping the tractor-wheel hurt
but the planting was a pleasure

As for the stiffness
it will fade

and think of the green
the cutting   baling   hauling

the machines waiting in a row
neat as knuckles

Remember last year
when we hauled bales

the binder-twine burnt like fire
through our gloves

That evening at the movie
we dared not tell each other

how much it hurt
to hold hands.

Union

MEG FISHER

If I marry
  there will be no frosting-sick cake,
  no curl-lettered namecards,
  no long-veil organ march,
  no red wet-eyed happiness,
  no silver-heavy gift tables,
  no sticky sweet mint tray,
  no life-watching minister,
  and no angel voices.
But the sun will leap
  as we run wild
        to windsung poems . . .
And the moon will pearl
  as we hum home,
            remembering.

Ascent

ADELE WISEMAN

Ascent is sheer delight,
but sudden birds must face
a danger of return
so swift it baffles flight.
And there, you'd think,
is where the skill comes in
to brake the dive,
but neither reflexes
nor timing can control
the throttle grip
of your hand on my heart
or my tailspin.
The perilous moment
for all high flyers
is the descent.

FIRST PERSON DEMONSTRATIVE

PHYLLIS GOTLIEB

I'd rather
heave half a brick than say
I love you, though I do
I'd rather
crawl in a hole than call you
darling, though you are

I'd rather
wrench off an arm than hug you though
it's what I long to do
I'd rather
gather a posy of poison ivy than
ask if you love me

so if my
hair doesn't stand on end it's because
I never tease it
and if my
heart isn't in my mouth it's because
it knows its place
and if I
don't take a bite of your ear it's because
gristle gripes my guts
and if you
miss the message better get new
glasses and read it twice

DISAPPOINTMENT

JEAN HILLABOLD

I waited for you
Until the avocados on my table
Turned to dust;
Until my curtains faded
From the heat of my stare;
And my feet wore down the carpet
And the wood under it;
Until my plants all died
And the cat ran away
To find a normal life;
Until my alarm clock exploded
And my fingernails became long knives;
Until the snow piled up to my third-floor windows.

I want you to know
That I moved to a better location
Where time trots faster.
I have a new Persian rug
And some healthy philodendrons
That complement my colour scheme.
The members of my Tuesday-night group
Are so witty
That I'm collecting their *bon mots*
With some of my sketches and photographs
For a book to be published in time for Christmas.
Do look for it.
My phone number is unlisted.
I don't give out my address
To just anyone,
And I'm rarely home.

If you tried to contact me, I wouldn't know it.
If you pounded on my door,
Sobbing my name,
The neighbours wouldn't recognize you
And would call the police.

You could have sent a letter to my old address,
Saying ''sorry,'' and ''please,'' and ''let me know,''
But it never reached me.

If I still cry sometimes;
If I still wear the necklace you gave me
In the hope of absorbing your strength,
The better to fight you
And to break hearts,
You never ask.
Your silence coats my walls
Like ice on rock.

EPILOGUE

DENISE LEVERTOV

I thought I had found a swan
but it was a migrating snow-goose.

I thought I was linked invisibly to another's life
but I found myself more alone with him than without him.

I thought I had found a fire
but it was the play of light on bright stones.

I thought I was wounded to the core
but I was only bruised.

I THOUGHT I SAW STARS

R.P. LISTER

I thought I saw stars, when first I saw your eyes,
So luminous they were, and such an enormous size;
I fell on the floor and foamed at the mouth, with inconsequential cries.

Now, when I look in your eyes, I do not flinch;
Heaven forgive me, I am not even tempted to lynch
The men who, standing beside you, display an inclination to pinch.

For this insensitivity may I be pardoned.
I looked in your eyes too often, and in the end became hardened;
There came a day when Adam turned his back upon Eve, and gardened.

A Heart That Has Been Broken

MAUREEN OWEN

A heart that's been broken
has a tiny hinge
And when it happens a
second or third time
it just
swings open & shut
like a gate.

To the Friend I Broke Up With

LYNNE FERGUSON

Life is a jigsaw puzzle
And people are the little pieces—
All different colours
And all different shapes and sizes.
Sometimes you pick up a piece
And match it with another,
And the colours blend perfectly,
And they fit into each other.
But in our case,
The colours clashed,
And the jagged little edges
Just wouldn't fit together,
No matter how hard we push them.
I guess we could have changed.
But isn't it against the rules
To cut up the pieces
so that they fit together

For Anne

LEONARD COHEN

With Annie gone
Whose eyes to compare
With the morning sun?

Not that I did compare,
But I do compare
Now that she's gone.

And This Is Love

PAULA REINGOLD

And this is love: two souls
That freely meet, and have
No need of proving anything;

No need of grasping, holding,
Forcing, and no need
Of needing: love is all.

It never can be satisfied,
Nor would it want to be—
Such love knows better than
To end itself. To satisfy
Would end it: let it be!

Then let us freely play
With all we have. Can lips
Kiss more than eyes? Two
Voices rise: could bodies mingle more?

This love brings harmonies
That fill the air:
We meet to celebrate,
And everything we do is love.

Oh, My Love

JOHN LENNON AND YOKO ONO

Oh, my love, for the first time in my life
My eyes are wide open
Oh, my love, for the first time in my life
I can see

I see the wind, oh, I see the trees
Everything is clear in my heart
I see the clouds, oh, I see the sky
Everything is clear in our world.

Oh, my love, for the first time
My mind is wide open
Oh, my love, for the first time
I can feel

I can feel sorrow, oh, I feel dreams
Everything is clear in my heart
I feel life, oh, I feel love
Everything is clear in our world.

Love Poem/*Robert Bly/p. 79*
Rewrite "Love Poem" using images from your own experiences. You might wish to make the poem longer and include some of the more unattractive or unpleasant things that are viewed differently through the eyes of love.

Love Is/*Ann Darr/p. 85*
What is your definition of love? Write a poem in which you share your view. You may imitate the tone and style of Ann Darr's poem if you wish. Choose or create a graphic to illustrate your poem. Arrange a class display of all the posters.

Union/*Meg Fisher/p. 88*
Prepare a monologue, lasting no more than two minutes, on the subject "If I marry." Instead of focussing, as Meg Fisher does, on what there will *not* be at the wedding, focus on what it *will* be like if and when you marry. You may choose to treat this topic in a serious or humorous manner.

Disappointment/*Jean Hillabold/p. 90*
Advice columns are a popular feature in many newspapers. Read several examples of the more popular advice columns to familiarize yourself with the style of the letters and of the responses offered by the columnist.

Write a "Dear Ann Landers" or "Dear Abby" letter. (Invent your own special columnist if you like.) Assume the identity of the speaker in either poem or of a friend of one of the speakers. Describe the situation as you see it and ask for advice.

Exchange letters with a classmate. Assume the identity of the columnist and reply to the letter.

And This Is Love/*Paula Reingold/p. 93*
Oh, My Love/*John Lennon and Yoko Ono/p. 94*
Which poem do you like best? Choose one and prepare a taped reading using appropriate background music. Share your reading with the class.

THE GREATER PERSPECTIVE

1. "If music be the food of love, play on . . ." Do you agree with Shakespeare's feeling that love and music go hand-in-hand? Make a list of current songs that deal with love in some way. Decide whether the songs have a positive or negative perspective on love. Transcribe the more relevant verses of the songs and create a "song book of love."
2. How important is love? Survey your friends and family to discover where they place love on a list of "The Ten Most Important Things in Life." Prepare a series of statements and a chart that illustrate the conclusions of your survey.

Chapter Six

6 The Pain of Earth-Bound Things

The world of dew
Is the world of dew.
And yet . . .
And yet . . .

ISSA

TRAGEDY

The transition from childhood innocence to adult knowledge is marked by a series of experiences that change our perspectives. Many of these experiences are pleasant; some, unfortunately, are not. Everywhere we look, we see evidence that people's lives are frequently touched by tragedy and pain.

Paul Zimmer, in the concluding poem of this chapter, suggests that the poet has a special healing power. Perhaps, by talking about death and loss, by asking questions and listening to others, and by reading poems written by people whose lives have been touched by tragedy, we can diminish our fears, our pain and our confusion.

There is no grief which time does not lessen.
SERVIUS SUPLICUS

> *The sorrow for the dead is the only sorrow from which we refuse to be divorced. Every other wound we seek to heal, every other affliction to forget; but this wound we consider it a duty to keep open; this affliction we cherish and brood over in solitude.*
> WASHINGTON IRVING

Light griefs can speak, great ones are dumb.
SENECA

> *He that lacks time to mourn, lacks time to mend.*
> SIR HENRY TAYLOR

As long as you can still be disappointed, you are still young.
SARAH CHURCHILL

Wild Geese

JOYCE DAVIS

I watched her clip their wings one day—
She said she'd keep them safe that way
From the dangers wild geese face
If they should leave this sheltered place.

And when that night I heard the cry
Of wild flocks soaring through the sky—
I shared the pain of earth-bound things
Held fast below on love-maimed wings.

Losings

SUZANNE JAY

The rescues were random.
They had to be.
When a fire is finally burning out of control,
it's not possible to prioritize possessions
by their value. All you can do
is snatch whatever happens to be lying close.
Because the important thing is to escape—
you and the child.

So things get left behind—
the baby book, the music box, the crystal
    hummingbird,
the prism that fractures colour all over a room.
And some of the child's things get left as well—
the ragged doll with only half her hair,
the bottle of magic bubbles, the stuffed frog,
the box of blue and green picture postcards.

Of course, as time passes
other things fill some of the empty places—
a racquet and blue ball, a painting of a sunrise, new
    books;
pop beads, sticker charts, glitter and glue.
But somehow the new things never quite fit the
    spaces
and it seems important to cry as I dust.

THE FYNCH COWS

ALDEN NOWLAN

The Fynch cows poisoned:
they'd torn the fence down,
gored one another for the befouled weed;

next day they bloated
and their bowels bled,
and they staggered crazily
around the miserly pasture—

John Fynch crying
as he stumbled after them,
with his rifle.

A RECOLLECTION

FRANCES CORNFORD

My father's friend came once to tea.
He laughed and talked. He spoke to me.
But in another week they said
That friendly pink-faced man was dead.

'How sad . . .' they said, 'the best of men . . .'
So I said too, 'How sad'; but then
Deep in my heart I thought, with pride,
'I know a person who has died.'

AS IN THE BEGINNING

MARY DI MICHELE

A man has two hands and when one
gets caught on the belt and his fingers
are amputated and then patched
he cannot work. His hands are insured
however so he gets some money
for the work his hands have done before.
If he loses a finger he gets a flat sum
of $250 for each digit &/or $100 for a joint
missing for the rest of his stay on earth,
like an empty stool at a beggar's banquet.
When the hands are my father's hands
it makes me cry although my pen must keep scratching
its head across the page of another night.
To you my father is a stranger
and perhaps you think the insurance paid is enough.

Give me my father's hands when they are not broken
and swollen,
give me my father's hands, young again,
and holding the hands of my mother,
give me my father's hands still brown and uncalloused,
beautiful hands that broke bread for us at table,
hands as smooth as marble and naked as the morning,
give me hands without a number tattooed at the wrist,
without the copper sweat of clinging change,
give me my father's hands as they were in the beginning,
whole,
open,
warm
and without fear.

Terry

LEONA GOM

The children running
running home
to be the first to tell:
''The tractor rolled over,
yesterday, yes, after school,
on the way to the field,
crushed him, yes.''
Eager with the disaster,
watching their parents greedily,
knowing that only such news
will make them pause—
hands for once still
on the unfinished fences,
on the axe incomplete over wood—
knowing that only such news
will make them look deeply
at their children,
see the fields and the farms
make their premature claim,
see their own children
dead under the overturned machines.

Stillborn

LORNA CROZIER

who
looped the cord
around his fine new neck

who
hanged him
in my bone gallows my
beautiful son
blue as the blue
in Chinese porcelain

THE PARDON

RICHARD WILBUR

My dog lay dead five days without a grave
In the thick of summer, hid in a clump of pine
And a jungle of grass and honeysuckle-vine.
I who had loved him while he kept alive

Went only close enough to where he was
To sniff the heavy honeysuckle-smell
Twined with another odour heavier still
And hear the flies' intolerable buzz.

Well, I was ten and very much afraid.
In my kind world the dead were out of range
And I could not forgive the sad or strange
In beast or man. My father took the spade

And buried him. Last night I saw the grass
Slowly divide (it was the same scene
But now it glowed a fierce and mortal green)
And saw the dog emerging. I confess

I felt afraid again, but still he came
In the casual sun, clothed in a hymn of flies,
And death was breeding in his lively eyes.
I started in to cry and call his name,

Asking forgiveness of his tongueless head.
. . . I dreamt the past was never past redeeming:
But whether this was false or honest dreaming
I beg death's pardon now. And mourn the dead.

EMPTY HOLDS A QUESTION

PAT FOLK

I saw him brought into Emergency,
reduced, behind his life-pressed scowl, to fear.
He'd been my teacher of geometry—
a tall, proud man behind a quizzing frown,
who'd pulled the theorems off the printed page
and called Infinity to being in my mind.
He'd said, "All things can be, quite logically,
defined with mathematics."
I was the one white uniform that wore a face—
he trusted me and signed the space that he'd refused before.
Presurgery, I took his pulse, all platitudes and hope . . .
But he did not return . . .
And so,
could not trace out for me
how I could be at twenty-two
as old as all mankind.

WHEN I HEARD OF THE FRIEND'S DEATH

JOHN NEWLOVE

When I heard of the friend's death in the mechanized city,
who was so clever, so young, so pleasant, I was ashamed

to be alive, all my faults in me, and him spoiled,
dirty and unreasonable at the accident's will.

Just so it is horrible to think of my father on his dead back
in the box, packed under dirt, his handsome face

falling apart. How curiously we deceive ourselves.

There is no consolation to be had anywhere for this.
There is always so much more to be said than can be said.

EMPTY HOUSE

STEPHEN SPENDER

Then, when the child was gone,
I was alone
In the house, suddenly grown huge. Each noise
Explained its cause away,
Animal, vegetable, mineral,
Nail, creaking board, or mouse.
But mostly there was quiet of after battle
Where round the room still lay
The soldiers and the paintbox, all the toys.
  Then, when I went to tidy these away,
My hands refused to serve:
My body was the house,
And everything he'd touched, an exposed nerve.

REUBEN BRIGHT

EDWIN ARLINGTON ROBINSON

Because he was a butcher and thereby
Did earn an honest living (and did right)
I would not have you think that Reuben Bright
Was any more a brute than you or I;

For when they told him that his wife must die,
He stared at them and shook with grief and fright,
And cried like a great baby half that night,
And made the women cry to see him cry.

And after she was dead, and he had paid
The singers and sexton and the rest,
He packed a lot of things that she had made
Most mournfully away in an old chest
Of hers, and put some chopped-up cedar boughs
In with them, and tore down the slaughter-house.

WAITING

PHYLLIS DAVIES

Why can't I stop

looking
at the sky . . .

watching
for the door . . .

listening
for your footsteps . . .

waiting
for your voice
smile
or touch?

How
many times
does my heart
have to flare with joy?

I see you,

then
it
falls,

s h a t t e r e d

on the floor

when I find
he's not you.

I see you
across the room,
down in the field,
roping in the arena,
running along the beach,
in a movie in the theatre,
biking along country roads,
blond hair tousled by the wind,
even wearing the jacket
you wore *that* day . . .

Sometimes
you are a little boy,
oftentimes a teen,
at times a man.
Yet always
my son.

It's

you

coming
down the street,
the Mother's Day
bouquet in hand,

the dozen
yellow roses
you so proudly
brought to me
this day last year.

I still can't believe
you are not coming home.

Today is Mother's Day.

GRIEF OF MIND

EDWARD DE VERE, EARL OF OXFORD

What plague is greater than the grief of mind?
  The grief of mind that eats in every vein;
In every vein that leaves such clots behind;
  Such clots behind as breed such bitter pain;
So bitter pain that none shall ever find,
What plague is greater than the grief of mind.

IS IT?

PHYLLIS DAVIES

Death isn't fair.

It isn't fair.

It isn't fair.

Is it?

YOUNG WOMAN AT A WINDOW

WILLIAM CARLOS WILLIAMS

She sits with
tears on

her cheek
her cheek on

her hand
the child

in her lap
her nose

pressed
to the glass

EROSION

E. J. PRATT

It took the sea a thousand years,
A thousand years to trace
The granite features of this cliff,
In crag and scarp and base.

It took the sea an hour one night,
An hour of storm to place
The sculpture of these granite seams
Upon a woman's face.

LAMENT

EDNA ST. VINCENT MILLAY

Listen, children:
Your father is dead.
From his old coats
I'll make you little jackets;
I'll make you little trousers
From his old pants.
There'll be in his pockets
Things he used to put there,
Keys and pennies
Covered with tobacco;
Dan shall have the pennies
To save in his bank;
Anne shall have the keys
To make a pretty noise with.
Life must go on,
And the dead be forgotten;
Life must go on,
Though good men die;
Anne, eat your breakfast;
Dan, take your medicine;
Life must go on;
I forget just why.

LAMENT

ANNE SEXTON

Someone is dead.
Even the trees know it,
those poor old dancers who come on lewdly,
all pea-green scarfs and spine pole.
I think . . .
I think I could have stopped it,
if I'd been as firm as a nurse
or noticed the neck of the driver
as he cheated the crosstown lights;
or later in the evening,
if I'd held my napkin over my mouth.
I think I could . . .
if I'd been different, or wise, or calm,
I think I could have charmed the table,
the stained dish or the hand of the dealer.
But it's done.
It's all used up.
There's no doubt about the trees
spreading their thin feet into the dry grass.
A Canada goose rides up,
spread out like a grey suede shirt,
honking his nose into the March wind.
In the entryway a cat breathes calmly
into her watery blue fur.
The supper dishes are over and the sun
unaccustomed to anything else
goes all the way down.

SUCCESS STORY

MARGARET ATWOOD

Please die, I said
so I can write about it.

THE FIVE STAGES OF GRIEF

LINDA PASTAN

The night I lost you
someone pointed me towards
the Five Stages of Grief.
Go that way, they said,
it's easy, like learning to climb
stairs after the amputation.
And so I climbed.
Denial was first.
I sat down at breakfast
carefully setting the table
for two. I passed you the toast—
you sat there. I passed
you the paper—you hid
behind it.
Anger seemed more familiar.
I burned the toast, snatched
the paper and read the headlines myself.
But they mentioned your departure,
and so I moved on to
Bargaining. What could I exchange
for you? The silence
after storms? My typing fingers?
Before I could decide, *Depression*
came puffing up, a poor relation
its suitcase tied together
with string. In the suitcase
were bandages for the eyes
and bottles of sleep. I slid
all the way down the stairs
feeling nothing.
And all the time Hope
flashed on and off
in defective neon.
Hope was a signpost pointing
straight in the air.
Hope was my uncle's middle name,
he died of it.

After a year I am still climbing,
though my feet slip
on your stone face.
The treeline
has long since disappeared;
green is a colour
I have forgotten.
But now I see what I am climbing
towards: *Acceptance*
written in capital letters,
a special headline:
Acceptance,
its name in lights.
I struggle on,
waving and shouting.
Below, my whole life spreads its surf,
all the landscapes I've ever known
or dreamed of. Below
a fish jumps: the pulse
in your neck.
Acceptance. I finally
reach it.
But something is wrong.
Grief is a circular staircase.
I have lost you.

THE NIGHT WILL NEVER STAY

ELEANOR FARJEON

The night will never stay,
The night will still go by,
Though with a million stars
You pin it to the sky,
Though you bind it with the blowing wind
And buckle it with the moon,
The night will slip away
Like sorrow or a tune.

Musée des Beaux Arts

W. H. AUDEN

About suffering they were never wrong,
The Old Masters: how well they understood
Its human position; how it takes place
While someone else is eating or opening a window or just
walking dully along;
How, when the aged are reverently, passionately waiting
For the miraculous birth, there always must be
Children who did not specially want it to happen, skating
On a pond at the edge of the wood:
They never forgot
That even the dreadful martyrdom must run its course
Anyhow in a corner, some untidy spot
Where the dogs go on with their doggy life and the
torturer's horse
Scratches its innocent behind on a tree.

In Brueghel's *Icarus*, for instance: how everything turns away
Quite leisurely from the disaster; the ploughman may
Have heard the splash, the forsaken cry,
But for him it was not an important failure; the sun shone
As it had to on the white legs disappearing into the green
Water; and the expensive delicate ship that must have seen
Something amazing, a boy falling out of the sky,
Had somewhere to get to and sailed calmly on.

"Good Night, Willie Lee, I'll See You in the Morning"

ALICE WALKER

Looking down into my father's
dead face
for the last time
my mother said without
tears, without smiles
without regrets
but with *civility*
''Goodnight, Willie Lee, I'll see you
in the morning.''
And it was then I knew that the healing
of all our wounds
is forgiveness
that permits a promise
of our return
at the end.

YOUR COUNTRY

GATIEN LAPOINTE
(translated by John Glassco)

If you will open your eyes
And if you will lay your hands
On the snow, the birds, the trees, the beasts,
Patiently, softly,
With all the weight of your heart;

If you will take time by the hand
And look upon the land
Patiently, softly;

If you will recognize your people
And if you recognize the pain
Trembling upon the background of their eyes;

If you will write the words love and loneliness
Patiently, gently,
On every season, every house;

If you will name bread, blood, day, night
And that wild unalterable desire
Burning at the heart of all things;

If you will take every death of your childhood
Patiently, softly, in your arms,
With all the strength of your despair;

Then your country can be born.

WHAT ZIMMER WOULD BE

PAUL ZIMMER

When asked, I used to say,
"I want to be a doctor."
Which is the same thing
As a child saying,
"I want to be a priest,"
Or
"I want to be a magician,"
Which is the laying
Of hands, the vibrations,
The rabbit in the hat,
Or the body in the cup,
The curing of the sick
And the raising of the dead.

"Fix and fix, you're all better,"
I would say
To the neighbourhood wounded
As we fought the world war
Through the vacant lots of Ohio.
"Fix and fix, you're all better,"
And they would rise
To fight again.
        But then
I saw my aunt die slowly of cancer
And a man struck down by a car.

All along I had really
Wanted to be a poet,
Which is, you see, almost
The same thing as saying,
"I want to be a doctor,"
"I want to be a priest,"
Or
"I want to be a magician."
All along, without realizing it,
I had wanted to be a poet.

Fix and fix, you're all better.

Losings/*Suzanne Jay*/*p. 99*
Imagine that the speaker in the poem is a close friend of yours. Write a sympathy note expressing how you feel about her loss. Offer words of encouragement and support.

Grief of Mind/*Edward de Vere, Earl of Oxford*/*p. 107*
The poet emphasizes the pain of ''grief of mind'' by repeating the last two or three words of each line at the beginning of the following line.

Write a poem in which you make use of this technique. Choose a subject (e.g., mourning, life, death, birth), then write a simple statement that says how you feel. Develop your statement in the same way as de Vere does.

Is It?/*Phyllis Davies*/*p. 107*
Transcribe this poem or write a variation of it onto a piece of poster paper. Find or create graphics to illustrate your poster.

Success Story/*Margaret Atwood*/*p. 109*
Imagine that the two lines of the poem were the last sentence spoken in a long conversation you once had with Ms. Atwood. Create the rest of the dialogue that went before this one sentence. (You might wish to write the dialogue as if you were a radio or television reporter conducting an interview.) Enlist the aid of a fellow student and tape your conversation.

THE GREATER PERSPECTIVE

1. On a piece of poster paper, create a collage made entirely of headlines from newspapers. Divide the poster in half. One half should serve to emphasize the prevalence of tragedy and loss in our world. The other half should illustrate that success, progress and happiness are also a part of our daily experiences.
2. The chorus in a popular Elton John song states that ''Sad songs say so much.'' Do you agree? Find a sad song that you think is particularly effective. Copy out the words to the song. In several paragraphs of personal writing, explain what the sad song says to you.

7 HIGH FLIGHT AND DARK CONCLUSIONS

There are two types of realists—
the one who offers a good deal of dirt with his potato,
to show that it is a real one;
and the one who is satisfied with the potato
brushed clean.

ROBERT FROST

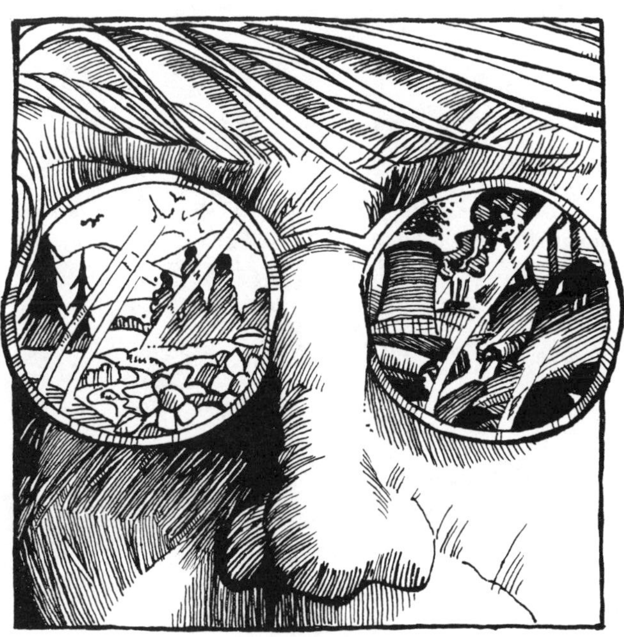

IDEALISM AND CYNICISM

How do you view life and people? Do you look at the world through ''rose-tinted'' glasses or through ''dark'' glasses? Are you an idealist, a cynic, or a little of both?

If you are an idealist, you probably believe that life, people, and the world can be improved. Idealists know that the potato in Robert Frost's quotation, no matter how dirty, can be brushed clean.

If you are a cynic, on the other hand, you probably believe that life, people and the world are in a worse state than they really are. Cynics, according to Frost, insist on offering a good deal of dirt with the potato to prove that it is a real potato.

How much dirt do you need to see on the potato? To what extent are you an idealist or a cynic?

I am an idealist. I don't know where I'm going,
but I'm on my way.
CARL SANDBURG

Cynicism is an unpleasant way of telling the truth.
LILLIAN HELLMAN

You must not lose faith in humanity. Humanity is an ocean; if a few drops of the ocean are dirty, the ocean does not become dirty.
MOHANDAS K. GANDHI

When there are two conflicting versions of a story, the wise course is to believe the one in which people appear at their worst.
H. ALLEN SMITH

HIGH FLIGHT

JOHN GILLESPIE MAGEE

Oh! I have slipped the surly bonds of Earth
  And danced the skies on laughter-silvered wings;
Sunward I've climbed and joined the tumbling mirth
  Of sun-split clouds—and done a hundred things
You have not dreamed of—wheeled and soared and swung
  High in the sunlit silence. Hov'ring there,
I've chased the shouting wind along, and flung
  My eager craft through footless halls of air . . .

Up, up the long, delirious, burning blue
  I've topped the wind-swept heights with easy grace,
Where never lark, or even eagle flew—
And, while with silent, lifting mind I've trod
  The high untrespassed sanctity of space,
Put out my hand and touched the face of God.

CITY HALL STREET

RAYMOND SOUSTER

In this sweet courtyard of dirt and smells and rot
children play, old men rock in their chairs, and women
hang out the ragged washings of the week. This goes on

winter, summer, fall and spring, year after year,
children playing, old men rocking, women washing,
only it is other children who play, other old men who sit in
    their chairs, other women hanging out clothes.

O this courtyard never changes,
it's still the same dirt, same rot, same smell,
same squirming, crawling tenement, tin-roofed sweat-box on
    the lower slopes of Hell,

open sore on the face of God.

To Satch

SAMUEL ALLEN

Sometimes I feel like I will never stop
Just go forever
Till one fine morning
I'll reach up and grab me a handful of stars
And swing out my long lean leg
And whip three hot strikes burning down the heavens
And look over at God and say
How about that!

Innocence

IRVING LAYTON

How does one tell
one's fourteen-year-old daughter
that the beautiful
are the most vulnerable
and that a rage
tears at the souls
of humans
to corrupt innocence
and to smash butterflies
to see their wings
flutter in the sun
pulling weeds and flowers
from the soil:
and that all, all
go under the earth
to make room for more
weeds and flowers
—some more beautiful than others?

[Untitled]

DAVID IGNATOW

If flowers want to grow
right out of the concrete sidewalk cracks
I'm going to bend down and smell them.

Passing Words

SUSAN GLICKMAN

Nothing is easy, that's what we're all saying,
the bruised lovers finding a laugh at the back
of anguish, the baffled parents muttering over how, how,
to say anything true
to the small ones whose nightmares are less frightening
than the world they wake to.
Trying to keep things clear. Trying to keep headlines
out of kitchens, to keep cancer from soup and bread,
bombs out of the bedroom. these
only the big ones
the ones so big they can't be seen; fiery starts
obscured by daylight and the atmosphere of earth
that startle us when night draws back
its curtains.
Usually it's the ordinary problems that won't let go,
that heckle and jeer behind the day's little triumphs—
failure of work, failure of play, failure
of love. But we all keep going, nothing
is easy we say, we say it
so easily.

THE WORLD IS A BEAUTIFUL PLACE

LAWRENCE FERLINGHETTI

The world is a beautiful place
to be born into
if you don't mind happiness
not always being
so very much fun
if you don't mind a touch of hell
now and then
just when everything is fine
because even in heaven
they don't sing
all the time

The world is a beautiful place
to be born into
if you don't mind some people dying
all the time
or maybe only starving
some of the time
which isn't half so bad
if it isn't you

Oh the world is a beautiful place
to be born into
If you don't much mind
a few dead minds
in the higher places
or a bomb or two
now and then
in your upturned faces
or such other improprieties
as our Name Brand society
is prey to
with its men of distinction
and its men of extinction
and its priests
and other patrolmen
and its various segregations
and congressional investigations

and other constipations
that our fool flesh
is heir to
yes the world is the best place of all
for a lot of such things as
making the fun scene
and making the love scene
and making the sad scene
and singing low songs and having inspirations
and walking around
looking at everything
and smelling flowers
and goosing statues
and even thinking
and kissing people and
making babies and wearing pants
and waving hats and
dancing
and going swimming in rivers
on picnics
in the middle of the summer
and just generally
'living it up'
Yes
but then right in the middle of it
comes the smiling
mortician

▲
The world has shown me what it has to offer . . .
It's a nice place to visit but I wouldn't want to live there.
ARLO GUTHRIE

FLIGHT ONE

GWENDOLYN MACEWEN

Good afternoon ladies and gentlemen
This is your Captain speaking.

We are flying at an unknown altitude
And an incalculable speed.
The temperature outside is beyond words.

If you look out your windows you will see
Many ruined cities and enduring seas
But if you wish to sleep please close the blinds.

My navigator has been ill for many years
And we are on Automatic Pilot; regrettably
I cannot foresee our ultimate destination.

Have a pleasant trip.
You may smoke, you may drink, you may dance
You may die.
We may even land oneday.

THURSDAY

WILLIAM CARLOS WILLIAMS

I have had my dream—like others—
and it has come to nothing, so that
I remain now carelessly
with feet planted on the ground
and look up at the sky—
feeling my clothes about me,
the weight of my body in my shoes,
the rim of my hat, air passing in and out
at my nose—and decide to dream no more.

LONE DOG

IRENE RUTHERFORD McLEOD

I'm a lean dog, a keen dog, a wild dog, and lone;
I'm a rough dog, a tough dog, hunting on my own;
I'm a bad dog, a mad dog, teasing silly sheep;
I love to sit and bay the moon, to keep fat souls
    from sleep.

I'll never be a lap dog, licking dirty feet,
A sleek dog, a meek dog, cringing for my meat;
Not for me the fireside, the well-filled plate,
But shut door, and sharp stone, and cuff and kick,
    and hate.

Not for me the other dogs, running by my side;
Some have run a short while, but none of them
    would bide,
O mine is still the lone trail, the hard trail, the best,
Wide wind, and wild stars, and the hunger of the
    quest!

▲

Afoot and light-hearted I take to the open road,
Healthy, free, the world before me,
The long brown path before me leading wherever I choose.
WALT WHITMAN

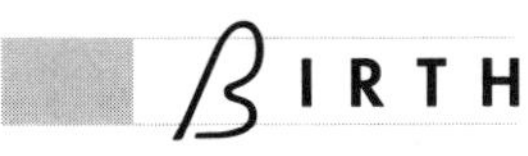

BIRTH

CÉCILE CLOUTIER

Perfect from the start
That small cell
Contains
Already
The wrinkles and death
Of an old man

YOUTH

FRANCES CORNFORD

A young Apollo, golden-haired,
  Stands dreaming on the verge of strife,
Magnificently unprepared
  For the long littleness of life.

THE WORLD'S SHORTEST PESSIMISTIC POEM

ROBERT ZEND

Hope?
Nope.

A SONG OF GREATNESS

MARY AUSTIN

When I hear the old men
Telling of heroes,
Telling of great deeds
Of ancient days,
When I hear that telling
Then I think within me
I too am one of these.

When I hear the people
Praising great ones,
Then I know that I too
Shall be esteemed,
I too when my time comes
Shall do mightily.

WISHES OF AN ELDERLY MAN AT A GARDEN PARTY

SIR WALTER RALEIGH

I wish I loved the Human Race;
I wish I loved its silly face;
I wish I liked the way it walks;
I wish I liked the way it talks;
And when I'm introduced to one
I wish I thought ''What Jolly Fun!''

THE PEACE OF WILD THINGS

WENDELL BERRY

When despair for the world grows in me
and I wake in the night at the least sound
in fear of what my life and my children's lives may be,
I go and lie down where the wood drake
rests in his beauty on the water, and the great heron feeds.
I come into the peace of wild things
who do not tax their lives with forethought
of grief. I come into the presence of still water.
And I feel above me the day-blind stars
waiting with their light. For a time
I rest in the grace of the world, and am free.

Lament

JON STALLWORTHY

Because I have no time
To set my ladder up, and climb
Out of the dung and straw,
Green poems laid in a dark store
Shrivel and grow soft
Like unturned apples in a loft.

Dark Conclusions

RUTH STONE

Like cutting the dry rot out of a potato,
There is nothing left in a moment but the skin
And a little milky juice. How awful to slice it open
And find the centre fustating, malevolent.

Standing on Tiptoe

GEORGE FREDERICK CAMERON

Standing on tiptoe ever since my youth
  Striving to grasp the future just above,
I hold at length the only future—Truth,
  And Truth is Love.

I feel as one who being awhile confined
  Sees drop to dust about him all his bars:—
The clay grows less, and leaving it, the mind
  Dwells with the stars.

MANY WORKMEN

STEPHEN CRANE

Many workmen
Built a huge ball of masonry
Upon a mountain-top,
Then they went to the valley below,
And turned to behold their work.
"It is grand," they said;
They loved the thing.

Of a sudden, it moved:
It came upon them swiftly;
It crushed them all to blood.
But some had opportunity to squeal.

FLORIDA ROAD WORKERS

LANGSTON HUGHES

I'm makin' a road
For the cars to fly by on,
Makin' a road
Through the palmetto thicket
For light and civilization
To travel on.

I'm makin' a road
For the rich to sweep over
In their big cars
And leave me standin' here.

Sure,
A road helps everybody!
Rich folks ride—
And I get to see 'em ride.

I ain't never seen nobody
Ride so fine before.
Hey, Buddy, Look!
I'm makin' a road!

THE COMPASS

GWENDOLYN MACEWEN

''Now Miss, the first thing you gotta understand
is that the earth moves around the sun.
I tell you this to help you get ahead in life.
And the next thing you gotta watch
your grammar, Miss, your grammar,
'cause that's important to get ahead in life.
And don't be afraid to face a big Congomeration of people,
me, I'm not afraid even though I just got out
of the Hospitality,
because I know where I stand, Miss,
and everything's gotta go and come back home
like the tides.''

''Now you give me a ship and I'll take her
to Germany or Africa, you name it
because I know how the Gulf Stream divides
the world in two,
and I'm not scared to cross the great Atitude;
yes Miss—Atitude—
they say the Atlantic but I know
it's the Atitude,
'cause you go down the Longitude to reach
the Atitude, you follow me?''

''Stars? Sure, I can sail by the North Star
and the South Star
and the East Star
and the West Star.
Even on this train, Miss
you don't know it but we be sailing
by those stars
'cause they're the compass points
for all the world.
See this compass, you turn five degrees
and then you come back home.
You gotta always come back home, Miss,
like the tides.''

"Look now, you be always at the centre,
even in a big Congomeration of people,
and all the words you talk here
go down to the sea, and the tide
brings 'em back tomorrow morning.
I tell you this so you won't fear
and you always know just where you stand
and how you're turning."

He turned the old German compass
over and over in his sure black hands.
"I had this fifteen years," he said,
"but I give it to you now so you
can get ahead in life,
and learn the Longitudes and Atitudes
and figure out just where you stand."

All I could think of
to give him in return
was my book of poems—a pointless gift.
But taking it he smiled and said,
"*I've* been doing some writing too
to get ahead in life!"
And pulled out from a suitcase old
as the crazy seas he sailed
something he handled with great respect—
a battered notebook where he'd written
in big scared lines
the first few letters of the alphabet.

STAR-GAZER

P. K. PAGE

The very stars are justified.
The galaxy
italicized.

I have proof-read
and proof-read
the beautiful manuscript.

There are no
errors.

from THE DIARY OF A YOUNG GIRL

ANNE FRANK

It's really a wonder
that I haven't dropped all my ideals,
because they seem so absurd
and impossible to carry out.
Yet I keep them,
because in spite of everything,
I still believe
that people are really good at heart.
I simply can't build up my hopes
on a foundation
consisting of confusion, misery, and death.
I see the ever approaching thunder,
which will destroy us too.
I can feel the sufferings of millions and yet,
if I look up into the heavens,
I think that it will all come right,
that this cruelty too will end,
and that peace and tranquillity will return again.

In the meantime, I must uphold my ideals,
for perhaps the time will come when I shall be able to carry them out.

FROM SEVEN AT NIGHT TILL FOUR IN THE MORNING

WALTER BAUER

From seven at night till four in the morning
I clean leftovers from plates and dishes
Into the garbage can,
Wipe glasses, silver plates, cutlery.
At nine my dreams are still fresh and shiny
And I could make the world a better place.
At midnight time drags itself across the steamed-up room
And lies down to die at my feet.

At two I hardly remember anything
And wipe the leftovers of my life
Into the garbage can.
At three I clean up the kitchen till it shines
In odourless light.
At four I step into the sharp lonely wind
And before the Milky Way fades
I drink from it my freedom.

NIGHT

YVONNE TRAINER

I was never afraid of the night
I'd sit on the farmhouse step and watch the stars
I'd count 5 up from the Big Dipper
to find the smaller one
the one with the bent handle
that leaked rain

I remember the white enamel dipper
that hung on a nail above the washstand
Mother polishing it once a day
Father chipping it when he threw it against the wall
in anger over something   I've forgotten
It doesn't matter

Still   light from the window
casts shadows over the yard
but the sky is calm
A whole universe
and nobody throws the stars
Everything has its place
    has order
Even the spaces belong.

TAKE SOMETHING LIKE A STAR

ROBERT FROST

O Star (the fairest one in sight),
We grant your loftiness the right
To some obscurity of cloud—
It will not do to say of night,
Since dark is what brings out your light.
Some mystery becomes the proud.
But to be wholly taciturn
In your reserve is not allowed.
Say something to us we can learn
By heart and when alone repeat.
Say something! And it says, "I burn."
But say with what degree of heat.
Talk Fahrenheit, talk Centigrade.
Tell us what elements you blend.
It gives us strangely little aid,
But does tell something in the end.
And steadfast as Keats' Eremite,
Not even stooping from its sphere,
It asks a little of us here.
It asks of us a certain height,
So when at times the mob is swayed
To carry praise or blame too far,
We may take something like a star
To stay our minds on and be staid.

(Untitled)/*David Ignatow/p. 121*
Imagine that these three lines of verse are part of a longer conversation and write the script of that encounter. Create a context for the dialogue. What are the speakers arguing about? What was said before these three lines? What was said afterwards? You might wish to use characters from other poems in this chapter as the "players" in your script.

Flight One/*Gwendolyn MacEwen/p. 124*
Rewrite the poem, having the Captain speak from the opposite perspective. How does changing the poem in this way affect your reaction to it?

The World's Shortest Pessimistic Poem/*Robert Zend/p. 126*
Robert Zend makes poetry writing look easy! Write a Zend poem. Choose a title similar in style to Zend's and create your own two-word rhyming poem. Remember that punctuation can add a world of meaning to your poem.

The Peace of Wild Things/*Wendell Berry/p. 127*
Write a poem or paragraph in which you describe vividly a place where *you* go to "rest in the grace of the world." Find or create an illustration to accompany your writing.

***from* The Diary of a Young Girl**/*Anne Frank/p. 132*
Imagine that a time machine has been invented that will deliver letters to anyone in the past.

Write a letter to Anne Frank in which you express how you feel about this particular entry. You may also wish to mention how things have turned out for the world since she wrote her diary.

From Seven at Night Till Four in the Morning/*Walter Bauer/p. 132*
A local service club has announced a new award scheme. They have decided to honour people in the community who display courage and optimism in their everyday lives and who set good examples for others to follow.

Imagine that you know the speaker in this poem very well. Write a letter to the service club, recommending that your friend be a recipient of this special award. Provide reasons for your recommendation. To create realism, you will need to invent specific details not provided in the poem.

THE GREATER PERSPECTIVE

1. Either
   a) Create a collage that illustrates the world as seen through the eyes of an idealist or a cynic;
   or
   b) contrast the two perspectives with one collage.
2. In 1516, Sir Thomas More published a book called *Utopia*. This was the name he gave to an island society where life was ''perfect.'' There was no crime, no poverty, and no injustice.

   Hold a class debate to decide whether such an ideal place could ever exist.
3. Prepare a questionnaire and conduct a survey of some of the students in your school to determine whether they are idealists or cynics. Tape, if you can, some or all of the interviews. Report your conclusion to the rest of the class.
4. What the eye behind a camera chooses to focus on will often reveal that person's sense of life.

   Create a video tape of your school and neighbourhood. Have your camera focus on objects and locations that make it obvious whether the camera-person is an idealist, a cynic, or a mixture of both.

8 LETTERS TO A FUTURE GENERATION

Above all I am not concerned with Poetry.
My subject is War, and the pity of War.
The Poetry is in the pity.

WILFRED OWEN

WAR

The history of the world has been marked by a succession of bloody conflicts and war. Past and present offer conclusive evidence that humanity is a violent species.

But does it always have to be this way? Are wars necessary?

Every generation has expressed its disapproval of war. Perhaps the times and our perspectives have changed to the point that we can finally discard the notion that war is heroic and full of glory. We realize that in the next World War, there will be no winners.

What do you think? Are we doomed to destroy ourselves and the planet through war? How realistic do you consider the hope that global peace and understanding can ever be achieved?

God forgive me but I enjoyed the war. Everybody's at their best during wartime. I'm sorry it's over.
THORNTON WILDER

War alone brings up to its highest tension all human energy and puts the stamp of nobility upon the peoples who have the courage to face it.
BENITO MUSSOLINI

I am tired and sick of war. Its glory is all moonshine.
GENERAL WILLIAM TECUMSEH SHERMAN

War is the supreme test of man, in which he rises to heights never approached in any other activity.
GENERAL GEORGE S. PATTON

Homo sapiens . . . are the biggest single menace to all living species on the planet earth.
PAUL D. HOLLOWAY

To jaw-jaw is better than to war-war.
WINSTON S. CHURCHILL

RUMOURS OF WAR

PAT LOWTHER

In my very early years
I must have heard
ominous news broadcasts
on the radio;
they must have mentioned
the Black Forest

for I dreamed a black forest
moving across a map,
I and my rag doll
caught on the coast edge
of the country
I was too young
even to name

Austria Poland Hungary
would have meant nothing
to me
but the Black Forest
came right up our ravine
down over the mountains

and Raggedy Ann
and I woke screaming
out of the clutch of
evil trees

FEE, FI, FO, FUM

EVE MERRIAM

Fee, Fi, Fo, Fum,
I smell the blood of violence to come
I smell the smoke that hangs in the air
Of buildings burning everywhere
Even the rats abandon the city
The situation is being studied by a crisis committee.

APOSTROPHE TO MAN

EDNA ST. VINCENT MILLAY

(on reflecting that the world is ready to go to war again)

Detestable race, continue to expunge yourself, die out.
Breed faster, crowd, encroach, sing hymns, build bombing airplanes;
Make speeches, unveil statues, issue bonds, parade;
Convert again into explosives the bewildered ammonia and
the distracted cellulose;
Convert again into putrescent matter drawing flies
The hopeful bodies of the young; exhort,
Pray, pull long faces, be earnest, be all but overcome,
be photographed;
Confer, perfect your formulae, commercialize
Bacteria harmful to human issue,
Put death on the market;
Breed, crowd, encroach, expand, expunge yourself, die out,
Homo called *sapiens*.

IF WE MUST DIE

CLAUDE McKAY

If we must die, let it not be like hogs
Hunted and penned in an inglorious spot,
While round us bark the mad and hungry dogs,
Making their mock at our accursed lot.
If we must die, O let us nobly die,
So that our precious blood may not be shed
In vain; then even the monsters we defy
Shall be constrained to honour us though dead!
O kinsmen! we must meet the common foe!
Though far outnumbered let us show us brave,
And for their thousand blows deal one death-blow!
What though before us lies the open grave?
Like men we'll face the murderous, cowardly pack,
Pressed to the wall, dying, but fighting back!

ONCE MORE UNTO THE BREACH

WILLIAM SHAKESPEARE

Once more unto the breach, dear friends, once more;
Or close the wall up with our English dead!
In peace there's nothing so becomes a man
As modest stillness and humility;
But when the blast of war blows in our ears,
Then imitate the action of the tiger:
Stiffen the sinews, summon up the blood,
Disguise fair nature with hard-favoured rage;
Then lend the eye a terrible aspect; . . .
Now set the teeth and stretch the nostril wide,
Hold hard the breath and bend up every spirit
To his full height! On, on, you noblest English,
Whose blood is fet from fathers of war-proof!
Fathers that like so many Alexanders
Have in these parts from morn till even fought,
And sheathed their swords for lack of argument.
Dishonour not your mothers; now attest
That those whom you called fathers did beget you!
Be copy now to men of grosser blood
And teach them how to war! And now, good yeomen,
Whose limbs were made in England, show us here
The mettle of your pasture. Let us swear
That you are worth your breeding; which I doubt not,
For there is none of you so mean and base
That hath not noble lustre in your eyes.
I see you stand like greyhounds in the slips,
Straining upon the start. The game's afoot!
Follow your spirit; and upon this charge
Cry "God for Harry! England and Saint George!"

DULCE ET DECORUM EST

WILFRED OWEN

Bent double, like old beggars under sacks,
Knock-kneed, coughing like hags, we cursed through sludge,
Till on the haunting flares we turned our backs,
And towards our distant rest began to trudge.
Men marched asleep. Many had lost their boots,
But limped on, blood-shod. All went lame, all blind;
Drunk with fatigue; deaf even to the hoots
Of gas-shells dropping softly behind.

Gas! GAS! Quick, boys!—An ecstasy of fumbling,
Fitting the clumsy helmets just in time,
But someone still was yelling out and stumbling
And flound'ring like a man in fire or lime.—
Dim through the misty panes and thick green light,
As under a green sea, I saw him drowning.

In all my dreams before my helpless sight
He plunges at me, guttering, choking, drowning.

If in some smothering dreams, you too could pace
Behind the wagon that we flung him in,
And watch the white eyes writhing in his face,
His hanging face, like a devil's sick of sin,
If you could hear, at every jolt, the blood
Come gargling from the froth-corrupted lungs
Bitter as the cud
Of vile, incurable sores on innocent tongues,—
My friend, you would not tell with such high zest
To children ardent for some desperate glory,
The old lie: *Dulce et decorum est*
Pro patria mori.

Remembrance

ALICE MAJOR

My father's brother went to war
 and died.
I have two photographs.

In one, a highland soldier stands
beside a tiny woman and laughs
into the sun.

I know her to be my grandmother.
His crisp-curled hair could well belong
to my own brother.

His arm is flung across her shoulder
his head thrown back. Details of sporran,
kilt, crests picked out distinctly
through the eye of a cheap camera
held by my father.

Impractical dress
in which to face the hot Egyptian sun,
the burning eye of death, the pain,
the blurring roar of guns,
the foreign desert sound,
El Alamein.

In the second photograph, ranks
of crosses march towards the camera,
their arms splayed, not quite touching,
regimented anonymity of death.
I cannot tell which one belongs
to the laughing soldier

"He lies beside a cousin of the queen,"
my father told me. He said it sadly,
as though even this did not confer
enough distinction on his brother.

from Five War Epitaphs

RUDYARD KIPLING

1. Common Form

If any question why we died,
Tell them, because our fathers lied.

FANTASIA

EVE MERRIAM

I dream
of
giving birth
to
a child
who will ask
"Mother,
what was war?"

VIMY UNVEILING

JOE WALLACE

How strange that grass
Should rise so green
From rains that fall
So red.

THERE WILL COME SOFT RAINS

SARA TEASDALE

War Time

There will come soft rains and the smell of the ground,
And swallows circling with their shimmering sound;

And frogs in the pools singing at night,
And wild plum-trees in tremulous white.

Robins will wear their feathery fire
Whistling their whims on a low fence-wire;

And not one will know of the war, not one
Will care at last when it is done.

Not one would mind, neither bird nor tree,
If mankind perished utterly;

And Spring herself, when she woke at dawn
Would scarcely know that we were gone.

FIVE WAYS TO KILL A MAN

EDWIN BROCK

There are many cumbersome ways to kill a man:
you can make him carry a plank of wood
to the top of a hill and nail him to it. To do this
properly you require a crowd of people
wearing sandals, a cock that crows, a cloak
to dissect, a sponge, some vinegar and one
man to hammer the nails home.

Or you can take a length of steel,
shaped and chased in a traditional way,
and attempt to pierce the metal cage he wears.
But for this you need white horses,
English trees, men with bows and arrows,
at least two flags, a prince and a
castle to hold your banquet in.

Dispensing with nobility, you may, if the wind
allows, blow gas at him, but then you need
a mile of mud sliced through with ditches,
not to mention black boots, bomb craters,
more mud, a plague of rats, a dozen songs
and some round hats made of steel.

In an age of aeroplanes, you may fly
miles above your victim and dispose of him by
pressing one small switch. All you then
require is an ocean to separate you, two
systems of government, a nation's scientists,
several factories, a psychopath and
land that no one needs for several years.

These are, as I began, cumbersome ways
to kill a man. Simpler, direct, and much more neat
is to see that he is living somewhere in the middle
of the twentieth century, and leave him there.

WORLD WAR III

EARLE BIRNEY

Will it be much as before?
Shall we learn to wear like fraternity pins
the deaths of our friends once more?
Will it be hard to keep track of the Finns
and who should be shot in the Balkans?
Of course we shall all play the rôle of the chicks
but who will be hooded like falcons?

Should youth as usual take the hint
politely declining to argue with print
permitted once more to gouge and smother
and mailed the weekly blessing from mother?
Will some save their money and some their lives
acquire new skills or noses or wives?

Shall we both fight superbly and sometimes with wrath
bemedal the brave and the bold psychopath,
the captains of industry, colonels or better,
the widow, the girl in the tightest sweater?

Will it be much as went by
with a leave between each slaughtering session
for movies where only the enemy die
and no time left to recall a depression?
When pulses and birth rates leap
when plagues are confined to the backward nations
and poets can ride in a jeep?

Or will it be more than before?
Will even Americans eat much less
restrict their water as well as their press
and bleed in the corner store?
Will all the old be killed
including the guilty, will space be filled
with blood like a Sunday paper?

Shall we all be scientists then and find
a method with plasma and plastic mind
to keep nearly everyone half-alive?
Shall we save humanely in leaden hive
our cretins, Creons, movable art,
and declared insane, for another start?

May we even dispense with the opening dream
of oldfashioned wars when we fancied the gleam
of a world sunrise, in the flash of the Sten
and peace was only postponed again?

Or will it be something quite new?
Before the pale clouds have cast their seed
before the twoheaded children succeed
can the brain teach the heart what to do?
Can love bend the earth to his will
can we kill only that which drives us to kill
and drown our deaths in a Creed?

from LOCKSLEY HALL

ALFRED, LORD TENNYSON

For I dipped into the future, far as human eye could see,
Saw the Vision of the world, and all the wonder that would be;

Saw the heavens fill with commerce, argosies of magic sails,
Pilots of the purple twilight, dropping down with costly bales;

Heard the heavens fill with shouting, and there rained a ghastly dew
From the nations' airy navies grappling in the central blue;

Far along the world-wide whisper of the south wind rushing warm,
With the standards of the peoples plunging through the thunder-storm;

Till the war drum throbbed no longer, and the battle-flags were furled
In the Parliament of man, the Federation of the world.

There the common sense of most shall hold a fretful realm in awe,
And the kindly earth shall slumber, lapped in universal law.

LETTER TO A FUTURE GENERATION

GWENDOLYN MacEWEN

we did not anticipate you, you bright ones
though some of us saw you kneeling behind our bombs,
we did not fervently grow towards you
for most of us grew backwards
sowing our seed in the black fields of history

avoid monuments, engrave our names beneath your own
for you have consumed our ashes by now
for you have one quiet mighty language by now

do not excavate our cities
to catalogue the objects of our doom
but burn all you find to make yourselves room,
you have no need of archaeology,
your faces are your total history

for us it was necessary to invent a darkness,
to subtract light in order to see,
for us it was certain death to know our names
as they were written in the black books of history

I stand with an animal at my left hand
and a warm, breathing ghost at my right
saying, Remember that this letter was made
for you to burn, that its meaning lies
only in your burning it,
that its lines await your cleansing fire—
understand it only insofar
as that warm ghost at my right hand breathed
down my blood and for a moment wrote the lines
while guns sounded out from a mythical city
and destroyed the times

Kid Stuff

December, 1942

FRANK HORNE

The wise guys
tell me
that Christmas
is Kid Stuff . . .
Maybe they've got
something there—
Two thousand years ago
three wise guys
chased a star
across a continent
to bring
frankincense and myrrh
to a Kid
born in a manger
with an idea in his head . . .

And as the bombs
crash
all over the world
today

the real wise guys
know
that we've all
got to go chasing stars
again
in the hope
that we can get back
some of that
Kid Stuff
born two thousand years ago.

Forget It

CAROLYN MAMCHUR

Star wars
Is no game.

In a nuclear war
Your nose drops off
And your dad
Never comes home
From work.

So who wants to play?

Imagine

JOHN LENNON

Imagine there's no heaven
It's easy if you try
No hell below us
Above us only sky
Imagine all the people
Living for today . . .

Imagine there's no countries
It isn't hard to do
Nothing to kill and die for
And no religion, too
Imagine all the people
Living life in peace.
Imagine no possessions
I wonder if you can
No need for greed or hunger
A brotherhood of man
Imagine all the people
Sharing all the world.

You may say I'm a dreamer
But I'm not the only one
I hope someday you will join us
And the world will be as one.

Fee, Fi, Fo, Fum/*Eve Merriam/p. 139*
Choose another nursery rhyme and write a parody of it in which you address an issue of current concern.

Apostrophe to Man/*Edna St. Vincent Millay/p. 140*
Imagine that you are an extra-terrestrial who has been studying humanity for many years. You know that, soon, there is bound to be another major global war.

Rewrite Millay's poem in the form of an objective report to be submitted to your home planet. Expand upon the items listed by Millay and provide specific examples of the human behaviour that has led to this imminent confrontation. You may retain Millay's pessimistic perspective or change it to a more optimistic one as you see fit.

In completing this activity, consider the fact that nowadays we try to avoid the use of "man" when referring to humanity.

Fantasia/*Eve Merriam/p. 144*
Imagine/*John Lennon/p. 149*
Transcribe either, or both, of the selections onto a large piece of poster paper. Identify the important images and feelings that the words suggest and illustrate these using material from magazines or your own artwork.

THE GREATER PERSPECTIVE

1. Write a poem on the subject of war. Decide which perspective you will adopt. Should your poem be through the eyes of youth? of age? of a soldier? of a pacifist? The poem should make a statement on how you feel about war.
2. Create a questionnaire to help you research attitudes towards war. Interview several individuals from various age groups and compare the results. Try to interview at least one war veteran. Tape record or video tape your interviews. Are there any general patterns in the way that most people view war?
3. Can you imagine a world ruled by peace? Write a concrete poem which illustrates what life would be like in such a world.

9 LET'S SKIP TRUTH TODAY

If you are a dreamer, come in,
If you are a dreamer, a wisher, a liar,
A hope-er, a pray-er, a magic bean buyer . . .
If you're a pretender, come sit by my fire
For we have some flax-golden tales to spin.
Come in!
Come in!

Invitation

SHEL SILVERSTEIN

DREAMERS

The focus of this chapter is on ''dreamers'' or those who, for one reason or another, choose to escape from the real world and life's problems or issues.

The selections emphasize that we become dreamers and escapists for a number of reasons. Sometimes we indulge in fantasies and daydreaming to avoid dealing with our innermost thoughts and feelings. At such times, we not only lock in our feelings, but we may also physically lock ourselves away from the rest of the world.

At other times, we might choose to escape to a dream world for short periods of time in order to enjoy the particular joys or pleasures to be found there.

Explore your attitudes and behaviours. To what extent are you a dreamer? How often do you choose to ''skip reality''?

The trouble with dreams, of course, is that
other people's are so boring.
W. H. AUDEN

Imagination is as good as many voyages—and
how much cheaper!
G. W. CURTIS

People are always blaming their circumstances for what they are. I don't believe in circumstances. The people who get on in this world are the people who get up and look for the circumstances they want, and, if they can't find them, make them!
GEORGE BERNARD SHAW

Dreams are the children of an idle brain
Begot of nothing but vain fantasy.
WILLIAM SHAKESPEARE

THE PROJECTIONIST'S NIGHTMARE

BRIAN PATTEN

This is the projectionist's nightmare:
A bird finds its way into the cinema,
finds the beam, flies down it,
smashes into a screen depicting a garden,
a sunset and two people being nice to each other.
Real blood, real intestines, slither down
the likeness of a tree.
"This is no good," screams the audience,
"This is not what we came to see."

SEEING MYSELF ON TV

LEONA DUBAY

Take the camera off
    the giggles
    the grin
the girl with short hair
  avoiding the camera's eye
    laughing at herself
      that's me?!
Why can't you let me alone?!
  look at someone else
wait a minute . . .
let me have just one more little glance
    let me see how others see me.
    No, let me out of that machine
I want to go back and sit at the table
      not in a box
  that's too educational
Send me back to my own little world
  let's skip truth today.

Mirrors

ELIZABETH BREWSTER

Mirrors are always magical.
So the child knows
who first sees one: the strange object
in which the other little girl appears
wearing the same dress, encircled in the same arms;
smiles, frowns, looks puzzled, cries, all the same
but somehow different.
For the other child does not have flesh, feels shiny to touch
and cold like the mirror's surface.
Mirrors are magic, and behind their surface
surely there is another Alice world
where you can walk and talk.

Mirrors are solid lakes,
and you could drown
beneath them if their outer layer cracked,
spin down and meet your real self far below,
a mermaid princess combing out your hair
before a magic mirror.

from Nicholas Knock

DENNIS LEE

Nicholas Knock was a venturesome boy.
        He lived at Number Eight.
He went for walks in the universe
        And generally got home late.

I SOMETIMES THINK

R. P. LISTER

I sometimes think I shall study to be a lama,
  I shall live by the difficult principles of Zen,
And devote my leisure moments to the Japanese drama,
    But I don't know when.

I sometimes think I shall lock myself in an attic
  And live on bread and water discreetly mixed,
Till life grows clear and my thoughts are pure and ecstatic,
    But the time's not fixed.

I sometimes think I shall go to the wide white beaches
  And lie in the sun till I cease to snuffle and cough;
There I shall learn what the palm tree says and the wild wave
  teaches.
    But I put it off.

I sometimes think I shall learn to play the sackbut,
  Or do research on the crystal structure of zinc,
In fact, I do very little but lie on my back, but
    I sometimes think.

FURROWS

DEBBIE PHILLIPS KUHNLEY

I am the plowhorse
Straining against the iron harness and leather whip
Dreaming of thoroughbreds
Running the meadows, nostrils funneling the scent of
    freedom and new growth
Pounding the distances, challenging the breeze which
    fans her mane.
I am the plowhorse, nose in a feedbag
dragging the ground,
Munching and dreaming of thoroughbreds.

THE PRINCESS IN THE TOWER

MARJORIE PICKTHALL

I was happier up in the room
At the head of the long blue stair
Than here in the garden's gloom
With roses to wear.

When stars my window were riming
I would lean out over the snow
And hear him climbing, climbing
A long way below.

But I was happy and lonely
As the heart of a mountain pool,
With stars and shadows only
Made beautiful.

Then he came. He said, "How chill is
This height I have won!
I will love you among the lilies,
And ride ere the sun."

So I followed him into the night
A long way down.
I would I were back on the height,
With dawn for a crown.

PSALM CONCERNING THE CASTLE

DENISE LEVERTOV

Let me be at the place of the castle.
Let the castle be within me.
Let it rise foursquare from the moat's ring.
Let the moat's waters reflect green plumage of ducks, let
the shells of swimming turtles break the surface or be
seen through the rippling depths.
Let horsemen be stationed at the rim of it, and a dog,
always alert on the brink of sleep.
Let the space under the first storey be dark, let the water
lap the stone posts, and vivid green slime glimmer
upon them; let a boat be kept there.
Let the caryatids of the second storey be bears upheld on
beams that are dragons.
On the parapet of the central room, let there be four archers,
looking off to the four horizons. Within, let the
prince be at home, let him sit in deep thought, at
peace, all the windows open to the loggias.
Let the young queen sit above, in the cool air, her child in
her arms; let her look with joy at the great circle, the
pilgrim shadows, the work of the sun and the play of
the wind. Let her walk to and fro. Let the columns
uphold the roof, let the storeys uphold the columns,
let there be dark space below the lowest floor, let the
castle rise foursquare out of the moat, let the moat be a
ring and the water deep, let the guardians guard it, let
there be wide lands around it, let that country where it
stands be within me, let me be where it is.

▲
Castles in the air—they're so easy to take refuge in.
So easy to build too.
HENRIK IBSEN

AN EARLY START IN MID-WINTER

ROBYN SARAH

The freeze is on. At six a scattering
of sickly lights shine pale in kitchen windows.
Thermostats are adjusted. Furnaces
blast on with a whoosh. And day
rumbles up out of cellars to the tune
of bacon spitting in a greasy pan.

Scrape your nail along the window-pane,
shave off a curl of frost. Or press your thumb
against the film of white to melt an eye
onto the fire escape. All night
pipes ticked and grumbled like sore bones.
The tap runs rust over your chapped hands.

Sweep last night's toast-crumbs off the tablecloth.
Puncture your egg-yolk with a prong of fork
so gold runs over the white. And sip
your coffee scalding hot. The radio
says you are out ahead, with time to spare.
Your clothes are waiting folded on the chair.

This is your hour to dream. The radio
says that the freeze is on, and may go on
weeks without end. You barely hear the warning.
Dreaming of orange and red, the hot-tongued flowers
that winter sunrise mimics, you go out
in the dark. And zero floats you into morning.

SPRINGSONG

ROBIN MATHEWS

I meet my son
(eleven years old)
running by me some blocks from home.
''Where are you going?'' I ask.
''Jogging'' he says,
matter-of-fact.

Altogether he has enough flesh to cover
about two grasshoppers.

But I understand
Snow's retreating fast.
Grass is showing,
even a few spiky crocus blades.
Mornings now the sun's in the twigs
flashing like swords.
Days start in an explosion of light.

I feel the way he does,
thinking every hour, these days,
of hopping a jet,
any jet,
and jogging away somewhere,
anywhere
or just staying up there in the blue
flying around

KEEP A HAND ON YOUR DREAM

X.J. KENNEDY

Keep a hand on your dream—
  Let it go too soon
And, though broad in the beam
  As a blown balloon,

It will dart all around
  Taking crazy trips,
Blowing spittle and sound
  From insulting lips.

I HAD A DREAM THAT TIME WAS A SAILBOAT

DEDE

I had a dream that time was a sailboat
I rented for a day
And with yesterday as my shadow
I set out to search for tomorrow
    me and time.
Rapping with the wind
And whispering secrets to the sea
As I shared a moment with the sun
My eye caught a glimpse of tomorrow
    out on the horizon.
I sat back and watched the new day stretching out ahead
Looking back I could see yesterday
Just a tiny dot on the shore
Where I left it only hours ago
I waved goodbye and focussed my attention on tomorrow
    now in full view.
As I approached I woke from my dream
Only to find that it wasn't tomorrow at all
It was just another day.

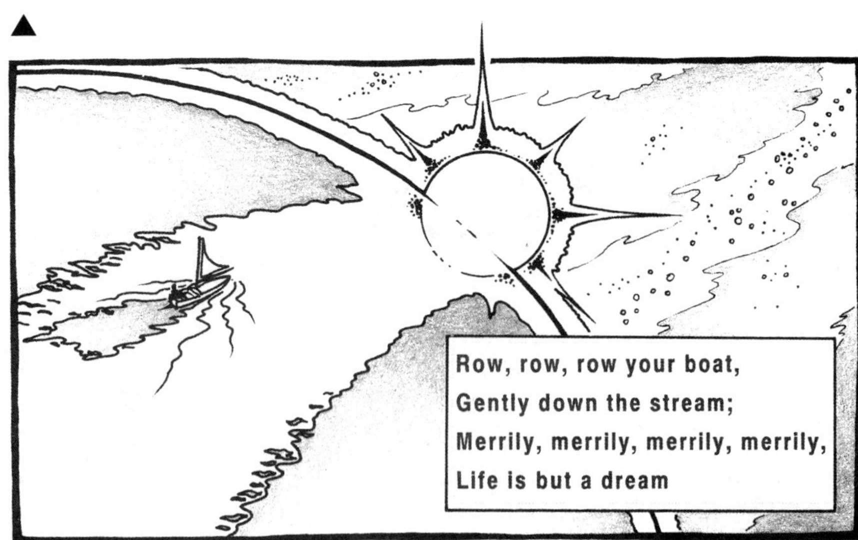

ON THE VALUE OF FANTASIES

ELIZABETH BREWSTER

The teacher on the morning radio program
disapproves because her girl students
have such unrealistic fantasies.
They all think they will go to college,
marry a lawyer or a professor,
have two kids and two cars,
and live happily ever after.

And she gets them to play a game
in which Linda becomes a widow at fifty,
Paulette is deserted at thirty-five
and has to bring up four kids
on a steno's salary, and poor Jennifer
never marries at all.
How will they cope?

Of course it's a matter of
one fantasy against another;
and sometimes it's fun
to imagine oneself bearing up against adversity.

Myself, though, I agree with the kids
that it's rather a dumb game.
It's true, life is full of these dirty tricks,
but being prepared for the worst may make it happen.

(More might be said
for fantasizing about space travel
or maybe about being a mermaid.)

I still hope (two months before my fifty-third birthday)
that I may yet meet that handsome stranger
all the fortunetellers have told me about;
that sometime my lottery ticket
will win a tax-free fortune,
and that my poems become household words
and make the next edition of Colombo's *Quotations*.

I might as well believe in heaven, too,
for all the good it will do me to admit
statistics are against it.

TO OLGA

ALENA SYNKOVA

Listen!
The boat whistle has sounded now
And we must sail
Out toward an unknown port.

We'll sail a long, long way
And dreams will turn to truth.
Oh, how sweet the name Morocco!
Listen!
Now it's time.

The wind sings songs of far away,
Just look up to heaven
And think about the violets.

Listen!
Now it's time.

PARADISE

CECILIA E. ALONSO

In the middle of tall dreamy woods, by the calm clear ocean, there sits a peaceful cabin.

As I allow myself to parade under the shade, to caress the hanging leaves, as I wrap myself onto a tree, I begin to experience freedom in paradise.

The breeze slowly finds its way into my hair. I slowly drop myself on a crisp meadow.

I share beautiful thoughts of peace, love, and serenity, with the flowers, the birds, and the wind.

The ocean has swallowed the chains, the cabin has locked away the pain.

I am free of body and mind.

WHO KNOWS IF THE MOON'S

E.E. CUMMINGS

who knows if the moon's
a balloon, coming out of a keen city
in the sky—filled with pretty people?
(and if you and i should

get into it, if they
should take me and take you into their balloon,
why then
we'd go up higher with all the pretty people

than houses and steeples and clouds:
go sailing
away and away sailing into a keen
city which nobody's ever visited, where

always
        it's
          Spring) and everyone's
in love and flowers pick themselves

THERE IS NO FRIGATE LIKE A BOOK

EMILY DICKINSON

There is no frigate like a book
  To take us lands away,
Nor any coursers like a page
  Of prancing poetry.
This traverse may the poorest take
  Without oppress of toll;
How frugal is the chariot
  That bears the human soul!

I GET HIGH ON BUTTERFLIES

JOE ROSENBLATT

I get high on butterflies:
the way they loom in the air
and land on air-dromes
          of petals

and with nervous wings
shake off their colours
          of orange, green and blue . . .

I get high on butterflies:
their very names:
    Tiger swallow tail
    Zebra
    Pygmy blue
    Arctic skipper
    Spring azure
    Common wood nymph.

Caught in the net of my mind
they whirl around
        and around . . .

Slow Guitar

EDWARD KAMAU BRATHWAITE

Bring me now where the warm wind
blows, where the grasses
sigh, where the sweet
tongued blossom flowers

where the showers
fan soft like a fisherman's
net through the sweet-
ened air

Bring me now where the workers
rest, where the cotton drifts,
where the rivers are
and the minstrel sits

on the logwood stump
with the dreams of his slow guitar.

Crazy Times

MIRIAM WADDINGTON

When the birds riot
and the airplanes walk,
when the busy sit,
and the silent talk;

When the rains blow
and the winds pour,
when the sky is a land
and the sea its shore,

When shells grow snails
and worms eat toads,
when winters chase summers
on upside-down roads,

We'll sit by our fires
and warm our hands,
and tell old tales
of bygone lands.

STAR-GAZE POEM

SANDFORD LYNE

In whatever galaxy,
I believe there must be creatures like ourselves,
dreamers,
savages,
poets,
builders of canoes,
far-scattered eyes moving
against the twinkling darkness of the heavens,
pilgrims
in equivalents of dust,
singers of small laments:
the ones we also know,
so well.

So,
for each such as me
this earth is enough of the possibility of grace.

I step out on my small porch, gaze:

these tiny lights, these beacons, bobbing
so far away in the night
we
cannot hear their bells
marking
the shallows of the universe.

The Projectionist's Nightmare/*Brian Patten*/*p. 153*
Imagine that you were in the audience at that movie theatre and the "nightmare" actually happened. Work with a partner and discuss what you saw as well as how you felt at the time.

Furrows/*Debbie Phillips Kuhnley*/*p. 155*
Kuhnley develops a contrast between how she actually sees herself and what she dreams of being. Write a poem in which you do the same. Choose an animal other than a plowhorse and describe yourself in terms of that creature. Indulge in a daydream. How could it *feel* to be that animal? Imitate Kuhnley's poem if you wish.

who knows if the moon's/*e.e. cummings*/p. 163
In groups of three or four, prepare a dramatic reading of the poem to share with the class. Organize the performance so that one or more of the group takes on responsibility for reading the poem while the remaining group members act out the images created by the words. You might wish to use props or costumes brought from home.

There Is No Frigate Like a Book/*Emily Dickinson*/p. 163
Much of the vocabulary used in the poem is unfamiliar to us because of the nineteenth-century diction. Make the poem more contemporary. Rewrite it using current vocabulary and a more modern mode of travel. You might even wish to substitute future forms of travel and take the poem into the 21st century.

I Get High On Butterflies/*Joe Rosenblatt*/p. 164
People get "high" on a variety of natural things. What kinds of things excite and exhilarate you?

Write your own "I Get High On Butterflies" poem. Use Rosenblatt's work as a model. Instead of "butterflies" deal with the particular thing that excites your imagination.

Once you have written your poem, transcribe it onto some colourful poster paper and find or create an illustration to go with the poem. Poems will be displayed on the bulletin board to be shared with the rest of the class.

THE GREATER PERSPECTIVE

1. Have you ever felt like shouting, "Stop the world, I want to get off!"? Write a short story in which you describe a day during which absolutely everything goes wrong. At one or more critical points in your story, have your protagonist drift into a "dream" sequence that somehow makes the unpleasant reality more bearable.

2. Have you ever thought about what your idea of paradise would look like? Write a poem or piece of prose in which you describe your idea of a perfect place. Use specific details and colourful images to convey a vivid presentation of your paradise. Find or create an illustration to go with your writing.

CHAPTER TEN

10 PROMISES TO KEEP

I go to encounter for the millionth time
the reality of experience
and to forge in the smithy of my soul
the uncreated conscience of my race.
from A Portrait of the Artist as a Young Man

JAMES JOYCE

INVOLVEMENT

There often comes a time when we appreciate the need for positive action and our own involvement with the world. We realize that some things are just too important to leave alone and we can no longer continue to allow things to happen around us without being "part of the action." We decide to become "doers" and follow through on the many promises—to life and to ourselves—that must be kept.

How involved are you with the world? Are you concerned with what is going on in your personal life, your city, your country, or your planet? Are you content to "take life as it comes?"

Action springs not from thought, but from a readiness for responsibility.
DEITRICH BONHOEFFER

All that is necessary for the forces of evil to win in the world is for good people to do nothing.
EDMUND BURKE

Action is the last resource of those who know not how to dream.
OSCAR WILDE

One never notices what has been done; one can only see what remains to be done.
MARIE CURIE

The only way to discover the limits of the possible is to go beyond them, to the impossible.
ARTHUR C. CLARKE

Sooner or later, everything becomes too important for someone else to handle.
RICHARD WEST

Work is much more fun than fun.
NOEL COWARD

DRIVING TO TOWN LATE TO MAIL A LETTER

ROBERT BLY

It is a cold and snowy night. The main street is deserted.
The only things moving are swirls of snow.
As I lift the mailbox door, I feel its cold iron.
There is a privacy I love in this snowy night.
Driving around, I will waste more time.

STOPPING BY WOODS ON A SNOWY EVENING

ROBERT FROST

Whose woods these are I think I know
His house is in the village though;
He will not see me stopping here
To watch his woods fill up with snow.

My little horse must think it queer
To stop without a farmhouse near
Between the woods and frozen lake
The darkest evening of the year.

He gives his harness bells a shake
To ask if there is some mistake.
The only other sound's the sweep
Of easy wind and downy flake.

The woods are lovely, dark and deep,
But I have promises to keep,
And miles to go before I sleep,
And miles to go before I sleep.

THE EAGLE

ALFRED, LORD TENNYSON

He clasps the crag with crooked hands;
Close to the sun in lonely lands,
Ringed with the azure world he stands.
The wrinkled sea beneath him crawls;
He watches from the mountain walls,
And like a thunderbolt he falls.

MIDNIGHT

ARCHIBALD LAMPMAN

From where I sit, I see the stars,
  And down the chilly floor
The moon between the frozen bars
  Is glimmering dim and hoar.

Without in many a peaked mound
  The glinting snowdrifts lie;
There is no voice or living sound;
  The embers slowly die.

Yet some wild thing is in mine ear;
  I hold my breath and hark;
Out of the depth I seem to hear
  A crying in the dark:

No sound of man or wife or child,
  No sound of beast that groans,
Or of the wind that whistles wild,
  Or of the tree that moans:

I know not what it is I hear;
  I bend my head and hark;
I cannot drive it from mine ear,
  That crying in the dark.

I SIT AND LOOK OUT

WALT WHITMAN

I sit and look out upon all the sorrows of the world, and upon all oppressions and shame,
I hear secret convulsive sobs from young men at anguish with themselves, remorseful after deeds done,
I see in low life the mother misused by her children, dying, neglected, gaunt, desperate,
I see the wife misused by her husband, I see the treacherous seducer of young women,
I mark the ranklings of jealousy and unrequited love attempted to be hid, I see these sights on the earth,
I see the workings of battle, pestilence, tyranny, I see martyrs and prisoners,
I observe a famine at sea, I observe the sailors casting lots who shall be kill'd to preserve the lives of the rest,
I observe the slights and degradations cast by arrogant persons upon labourers, the poor, and upon Negroes, and the like;
All these—all the meanness and agony without end I sitting look out upon,
See, hear, and am silent.

OF CATS AND BELLS

SUNITI NAMJOSHI

''Who will bell the cat?'' ''Not I,'' said the Brown Mouse,
''I have too many babies, and a hundred things to do,
and a long shopping list.'' ''Not I,'' said the Blue
Mouse, ''I hate silly fights, and I believe in peace.'' ''Not
I,'' said the Little Mouse, ''I am too little, and the
bell is too heavy.'' ''Nor I,'' said the Big Mouse, ''I do
not understand the nature of bells, and moreover,
they bore me.'' ''Well, I'll bell the cat,'' said the Lunatic
Mouse, ''I'll do it for a lark. It's really quite funny.''
''No, I'll bell the cat,'' said the Heroic Mouse, ''I want
the glory.'' ''If we wait long enough,'' said the Clever
Mouse, ''the cat will die, and then we needn't worry.''
''Yes,'' said the mice, ''let us forget it''; and some
didn't and some did.

IT IS DANGEROUS TO READ NEWSPAPERS

MARGARET ATWOOD

While I was building neat
castles in the sandbox,
the hasty pits were
filling with bulldozed corpses

and as I walked to the school
washed and combed, my feet
stepping on the cracks in the cement
detonated red bombs.

Now I am grownup
and literate, and I sit in my chair
as quietly as a fuse

and the jungles are flaming, the under-
brush is charged with soldiers,
the names on the difficult
maps go up in smoke.

I am the cause, I am a stockpile of chemical
toys, my body
is a deadly gadget,
I reach out in love, my hands are guns,
my good intentions are completely lethal.

Even my
passive eyes transmute
everything I look at to the pocked
black and white of a war photo,
how
can I stop myself

It is dangerous to read newspapers.

Each time I hit a key
on my electric typewriter,
speaking of peaceful trees

another village explodes.

RETURNING TO THE WORLD

BARBARA CAREY

I know this sadness
that I'm sunk in
is just like any other
& will pass—
but for now it rises
with all the senseless
waste of the world, the surplus
greed & shortages of caring,
& sends me from friends' arms
to sit fiercely
alone on the fire escape

I remember my father
hunched over on the bottom
step of the back stairs,
out of reach
of the frayed light
nibbling at the end
of its single cord

don't bother him, he's
thinking, my mother said,
knowing that tiredness
clings too, like mud
caked on a pair
of boots or darkness
to the steep sides
of a well
he'll come up
when he's ready

I don't know why
stairs are for deep
thinking, they just are—
maybe it's the solid
wedge of up & down
level against the spine,
or that the banister
is a ladder of arms
to give us rest

& then to pull
us up again, the way
a bucket is raised
swinging clear
water up from a
well's depths,
hand over hand
something to hold
onto, returning
to the world

PREPAREDNESS

EDWIN MARKHAM

For all your days prepare,
  And meet them ever alike:
When you are the anvil, bear—
  When you are the hammer, strike.

TEARS ARE NOT ENOUGH

BRYAN ADAMS, DAVID FOSTER, and JIM VALLANCE

As every day goes by
How can we close our eyes
Until we open up our hearts?
We can learn to share
And show how much we care
Right from the moment that we start.
Seems like overnight
We see the world in a diff'rent light.
Somehow our innocence is lost.
How can we look away
'Cause ev'ry single day
We got to help at any cost.

CHORUS
We can bridge the distance;
Only we can make the diff'rence.
Don't you know that tears are not enough.
If we can pull together
We can change the world forever.
Heaven knows that tears
are not enough.

It's up to me and you
To make the dream come true.
It's time to take our message everywhere,
You know . . .
C'est l'amour qui nous rassemble
D'ici a l'autre bout du monde.
Let's show them Canada still cares.
You know that we'll be there.

CHORUS

And if we should try, together you and I,
Maybe we could understand the reasons why.
If we take a stand, ev'ry woman, child and man,
We can make it work.
For God sake, lend a hand.

CHORUS

LEONARDO

NELLIE McCLUNG

The time will come when men
will look upon the murder
of animals as they do of men.
Leonardo da Vinci

Even in the days
of his poverty,
the vegetarian genius
bought birds in the
market place, to set them
free

like Pythagoras
before him
& Montaigne

▲
When will we reach the point that hunting,
the pleasure in killing animals for sport,
will be regarded as a mental aberration?
When will all the killing that necessity imposes upon us
be undertaken with sorrow?
ALBERT SCHWEITZER

THE DRUM

NIKKI GIOVANNI

daddy says the world is
a drum tight and hard
and I told him
I'm gonna beat
out my own rhythm

L'ORIGNAL

R.G. EVERSON

The bull moose only a startling rod or so away from me
looked to be about nine feet long
maybe six feet above the trampled-down snow
and he would go about a thousand pounds
even though starved gaunt. He was murder-angry had eaten
all the undergrowth and above him all twigs and branches
within reach so that the little forest on his island was
trimmed
evenly along the lower parts of the trees
according to the undulations of the land

This mini-skirts appearance of the island had drawn my
curiosity
as I crossed the lake on the way home with the new axe—
to encounter the terrifying sight at close range of *l'orignal*
as the French long ago named the bull moose having never
seen so strange an animal in Europe (The Indians called
him mongswa
from which the English took the name the twig eater)

The moose had probably been chased to this island
in the deep of winter. Nearby me on the lake ice lay a long-
dead wolf
(on a guess, a wolf—I hadn't seen one outside a museum or zoo)
frozen at full stretch and partly drifted over.
I figured that the moose had used the small island as a fort
Even after the wolves gave up and went away
the moose may have stayed browsing but the island had
trapped him

The ice shore had become too weak for a getaway
The late winter sun heating shore rocks
had circled the island with a thin-crusted moat. I observed
where the starving moose had several times broken through
in trying to escape after he had eaten everything within reach
Dimly seeing me out here among pressure ridges
and water pools in the sugar snow over yard-deep ice
the moose probably took me for one of those wolves
so he charged

Immediately he splintered through the ice and disappeared
When he came up on a tide of icicles and water
he kept on trying to get at me slamming
the breaking ice with his forelegs. He had no horns.
I however was having a close look at his front hooves
until he turned around and feebly swam through ice-floes
He was a long time dragging himself up over the shore rocks.

I walked half-way around his little island
and bellied over the thin ice pushing
my axe ahead of me. I didn't quite break through
and ashore quickly inexpertly cut down a poplar
pushing it inland as the moose staggered toward me
The falling treetop confronted his weak charge. The
monster
began to nibble on the delicate twigs
In March all deer are starving and weak but this one
was the prize woebegone. His bell was thin as a string

He stayed at the end of the tree and kept eating
while I managed to hack down another poplar and another
ruining our environment and probably breaking some laws
but there was peace between that moose and me. I worked
until I figured that he had fodder enough for break-up
when he could get off the island and swim to a mainland
forest for a fresh start. Then I crawled full length
over the weak shore ice and walked along the lake
in the last of the late-winter day

BE QUIET, STAND STILL

VIRGINIA C. ABBOTT

''Be quiet, stand still.''
And, I thought . . .
Water doesn't stand still,
Clouds don't stay still—
And,
Leaves on trees don't stand still.
Just all kinds of things—
Don't stand or stay still.

LUCINDA MATLOCK

EDGAR LEE MASTERS

I went to dances at Chandlerville,
And played snap-out at Winchester.
One time we changed partners,
Driving home in the moonlight of middle June,
And then I found Davis.
We were married and lived together for seventy years,
Enjoying, working, raising the twelve children,
Eight of whom we lost
Ere I had reached the age of sixty.
I spun, I wove, I kept the house, I nursed the sick,
I made the garden, and for holiday
Rambled over the fields where sang the larks,
And by Spoon River gathering many a shell,
And many a flower and medicinal weed—
Shouting to the wooded hills, singing to the green valleys.
At ninety-six I had lived enough, that is all,
And passed to a sweet repose.
What is this I hear of sorrow and weariness,
Anger, discontent, and drooping hopes?
Degenerate sons and daughters,
Life is too strong for you—
It takes life to love Life.

MAKING SENSE

PIET HEIN

Life makes sense,
and who could doubt it,
if we have
no doubt about it.

FOR I MUST GO

MICHAEL BULLOCK

If that is my destiny,
so be it.
Whether the journey leads to death
or joy
it must be made.
Immobility is the only cardinal sin,
to remain static the unforgivable crime.
Movement is life,
no matter where we go.

I Sit and Look Out/*Walt Whitman/p. 173*
Look around you and, like Whitman, "see and hear" the sorrows of the world. Write an "I Sit and Look Out" poem, imitating Whitman's style if you wish. Tape record a reading of your poem accompanied by appropriate background music.

Of Cats and Bells/*Suniti Namjoshi/p. 173*
Prepare a dramatic reading of this poem. You will need up to nine readers. You may use props or costumes to characterize the different mice. If possible, video tape your presentation.

Leonardo/*Nellie McClung/p. 177*
Try either of these projects.
a) Leonardo da Vinci, Pythagoras, and Montaigne shared a strong belief—that birds and animals have the right to be free. Research the life of one of these men, focussing on this particular aspect. Report your findings to the class;
b) Imagine you are Leonardo and that you are, at the moment, especially broke. Write the script for a conversation during which you ask a friend for money so that you can buy some birds. Enlist the help of a friend and present your dialogue to the class.

Be Quiet, Stand Still/*Virginia C. Abbott/p. 179*
Imagine that you are the speaker in the poem. Write the diary entry you made the day that this conversation took place. You will need to describe the events of the day that preceded the conversation. You might also wish to deal with what happened after the conversation took place.

For I Must Go/*Michael Bullock/p. 180*
Transcribe the poem onto a piece of poster paper. Then reread the poems and quotations in this chapter, selecting lines that are especially meaningful to you. Write these on the poster paper as well.

Using pictures from newspapers, magazines, and/or your own imagination, create a series of collages to illustrate the ideas and feelings suggested by the words.

THE GREATER PERSPECTIVE

1. With a partner, compile a list of ten individuals who you consider are, or were, truly involved in making their community/the world a better place in which to live. Beside each name, list one or more important personality traits for each individual and summarize briefly his or her most important accomplishments.
2. Choose a ''doer'' either from history or the present day, and write the script of an imaginary interview with that person as it might appear on a popular evening talk show. The questions and answers should focus on the theme of responding to the ''sorrows of the world.''
3. Write a letter of thanks and appreciation to an individual who you think has shown a deep commitment to making this world a better place to live. Enlist the aid of your librarian in searching out the address of this person. Mail the final draft of your letter. Report to the class if you receive a reply.

CHAPTER ELEVEN

11 TO SEE THE EARTH AS IT TRULY IS

To see the earth as it truly is—
small and blue and beautiful in that
eternal silence where it floats, is to see
ourselves as riders on the earth together.

ARCHIBALD MACLEISH

NATURE AND THE ENVIRONMENT

Poetry has always been concerned with nature. So many poems have been, and are being, written on the subject of flowers and trees, rainbows, and sunshine, mountains and oceans, forests and gardens, that these areas seem to be the undisputed domain of verse.

Today, poets are once again focussing on nature. Nature worship, however, has been replaced by the increasing fear, horror and concern that we may be seeing the death of our natural environment in the not too distant future.

How real is the threat to our planet's environment?

Old Mother Hubbard went to the cupboard
To fetch her poor dog a bone
But when she got there the cupboard was bare
And so the poor dog had none.
TRADITIONAL NURSERY RHYME

What use is a house, if you haven't got a tolerable planet to put it on?
HENRY DAVID THOREAU

Litter is a disgusting way of proving your affluence.
SIR HENRY BOLTE

We're now living 200 years per annum. When you're moving at that clip there's no place to stand. It's like putting a Model T on the highway at 100 mph. It breaks down.
MARSHALL McLUHAN

We have lost the sense of belonging to the environment, and behave as if the environment belonged to us. But we are neither superior to, nor independent of, our environment; we are a part of it.
ASHLEY MONTAGU

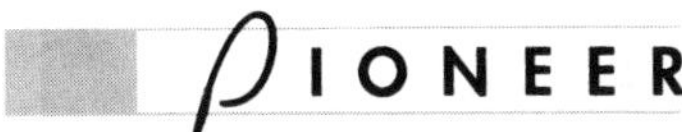

PIONEER

DOROTHY LIVESAY

He laboured, starved, and ploughed:
In these last days
Cities roar where his voice
In lonely wilderness first sang out praise.

Out of the forest, walls,
From rock, the wheat:
Winters to chill the heart
That slowly withers in the summer's heat.

Out of the fight, desire
Re-born each spring
To leave some mark behind—
High harvest for the autumn's gathering.

What labourer could dream
The axe's chime
And swiftly builded house
Would mean a city in so brief a time . . .

He sits with folded hands
And burns to see
How he has ravaged earth
Of her last stone, her last, most stubborn tree.

PROGRESS?

HUBERT EVANS

When he was a boy
he worked with his father in the woods.

When he had a boy
they walked in the woods of a Sunday.

Now that boy has a boy.
But the woods are gone.

IF A TREE FALLS

BRUCE COCKBURN

rain forest
mist and mystery
teeming green
green brain facing lobotomy
climate control centre for the world
ancient cord of coexistence
hacked by parasitic greedhead scam—
from Sarawak to Amazonas
Costa Rica to mangy B.C. hills—
cortege rhythm of falling timber.

What kind of currency grows in these new deserts.
these brand new flood plains?

If a tree falls in the forest does anybody hear?
If a tree falls in the forest does anybody hear?
Anybody hear the forest fall?

Cut and move on
Cut and move on
take out trees
take out wildlife at a rate of a species every
single day
take out people who've lived with this for 100 000
years—
inject a billion burgers worth of beef—
grain eaters—methane dispensers—

through thinning ozone.
waves fall on wrinkled earth—
gravity, light, ancient refuse of stars.
speak of a drowning—
but this, this is something other
busy monster eats dark holes in the spirit world
where wild things have to go
to disappear
forever

If a tree falls in the forest, does anybody hear?
If a tree falls in the forest, does anybody hear?
Anybody hear the forest fall?

DEFORESTATION

SCOTT KEEDWELL

T T T T T T

R R R R R R

E E E E E E

E E E E E E

E R E T

THE WORLD IS TOO MUCH WITH US

WILLIAM WORDSWORTH

The world is too much with us; late and soon,
Getting and spending, we lay waste our powers:
Little we see in Nature that is ours;
We have given our hearts away, a sordid boon!
This sea that bares her bosom to the moon;
The winds that will be howling at all hours,
And are up-gathered now like sleeping flowers;
For this, for everything, we are out of tune;
It moves us not. Great God! I'd rather be
A pagan suckled in a creed outworn;
So might I, standing on this pleasant lea,
Have glimpses that would make me less forlorn;
Have sight of Proteus rising from the sea;
Or hear old Triton blow his wreathèd horn.

THE WALRUS AND THE CARPENTER

LEWIS CARROLL

The sun was shining on the sea,
Shining with all his might:
He did his very best to make
The billows smooth and bright—
And this was odd, because it was
The middle of the night.

The moon was shining sulkily,
Because she thought the sun
Had got no business to be there
After the day was done—
"It's very rude of him," she said,
"To come and spoil the fun!"

The sea was wet as wet could be,
The sands were dry as dry.
You could not see a cloud, because
No cloud was in the sky:
No birds were flying overhead—
There were no birds to fly.

The Walrus and the Carpenter
Were walking close at hand;
They wept like anything to see
Such quantities of sand:
"If this were only cleared away,"
They said, "it *would* be grand!"

"If seven maids with seven mops
Swept it for half a year,
Do you suppose," the Walrus said,
"That they could get it clear?"
"I doubt it," said the Carpenter,
And shed a bitter tear.

"O Oysters, come and walk with us!"
The Walrus did beseech.
"A pleasant walk, a pleasant talk,
Along the briny beach:
We cannot do with more than four,
To give a hand to each."

The eldest Oyster looked at him,
  But not a word he said:
The eldest Oyster winked his eye,
  And shook his heavy head—
Meaning to say he did not choose
  To leave the oyster-bed.

But four young Oysters hurried up,
  All eager for the treat:
Their coats were brushed, their faces washed,
  Their shoes were clean and neat—
And this was odd, because, you know,
  They hadn't any feet.

Four other Oysters followed them,
  And yet another four;
And thick and fast they came at last,
  And more, and more, and more—
All hopping through the frothy waves,
  And scrambling to the shore.

The Walrus and the Carpenter
  Walked on a mile or so,
And then they rested on a rock
  Conveniently low:
And all the little Oysters stood
  And waited in a row.

"The time has come," the Walrus said,
  "To talk of many things:
Of shoes—and ships—and sealing wax—
  Of cabbages—and kings—
And why the sea is boiling hot—
  And whether pigs have wings."

"But wait a bit," the Oysters cried,
  "Before we have our chat;
For some of us are out of breath,
  And all of us are fat!"
"No hurry!" said the Carpenter.
  They thanked him much for that.

''A loaf of bread,'' the Walrus said,
  ''Is what we chiefly need:
Pepper and vinegar besides
  Are very good indeed—
Now, if you're ready, Oysters dear,
  We can begin to feed.''

''But not on us!'' the Oysters cried,
  Turning a little blue.
''After such kindness that would be
  A dismal thing to do!''
''The night is fine,'' the Walrus said,
  ''Do you admire the view?''

''It was so kind of you to come,
  And you are very nice!''
The Carpenter said nothing but
''Cut us another slice.
I wish you were not quite so deaf—
  I've had to ask you twice!''

''It seems a shame,'' the Walrus said,
  ''To play them such a trick.
After we've brought them out so far
  And made them trot so quick!''
The Carpenter said nothing but
  ''The butter's spread too thick!''

''I weep for you,'' the Walrus said,
  ''I deeply sympathize.''
With sobs and tears he sorted out
  Those of the largest size,
Holding his pocket-handkerchief
  Before his streaming eyes.

''O Oysters,'' said the Carpenter,
  ''You've had a pleasant run!
Shall we be trotting home again?''
  But answer came there none—
And this was scarcely odd, because
  They'd eaten every one.

"I like the Walrus best," said Alice: "because he was a *little* sorry for the poor oysters."

"He ate more than the Carpenter, though," said Tweedledee. "You see he held his handkerchief in front, so that the Carpenter couldn't count how many he took: contrariwise."

"That was mean!" Alice said indignantly. "Then I like the Carpenter best—if he didn't eat so many as the Walrus."

"But he ate as many as he could get," said Tweedledum.

This was a puzzler. After a pause, Alice began, "Well! They were *both* very unpleasant characters—"

Why, then, the world's mine oyster
Which I with sword will open.
WILLIAM SHAKESPEARE

BY WAY OF ERROR

CÉCILE CLOUTIER

Man
Has turned sails
One
By
One
And read
The big blue page
Of the sea

Then
He has built up
Some thousands
Of millions
Of miles
Of light cables

And he has given them
Some millions
Of thousands
Of knots

All to tie up the sea

SEVEN DAYS

GARY DUNFORD

in the beginning,
man created the mudhole and the marsh
  damming streams for viaducts
  and routing waters for his own benefit
    waters, white as crystal, moving through trenches
    trickling through makeshift reed piping
    splashing clean into clay bowls
    bubbling to do man's bidding
  and it was the morning and the evening of the first day
  and the seagulls were dying

on the second day,
man created the slaughterhouse and the zoo
  and the wild animals of the earth
  which had wandered at will across the planet
    watched man from behind wire mesh
    scruffy lions with sad faces
    and elephants, their bottoms calloused from sitting on cement
  and it was the morning and the evening of the second day
  and the seagulls were dying

on the third day,
the buffalo disappeared. simply disappeared.
  and across the pampas
  safaris, $495 per person, sought out exotic creatures
  to mount in rec rooms or multiply in cages
    and the ice floes ran red
    and the jungle monkeys reeled in terror
  and it was the morning and the evening of the third day
  and the seagulls were dying

on the fourth day,
man created the sewer and the sump
  and pumps to pipe sewer to sump and sump to sewer at incredible
  cost
    to nose and pocket
  and the pumps pumped
  and the sumps drained
  and the sewers flowed
  into creeks and lakes

and every drop of sewage makes
an ocean spreading across the world
the universal garbage apocalypse
and it was the morning and the evening of the fourth day
and the seagulls were dying

on the fifth day,
man crated and canned atomic wastes
and made up the word megaton
packing the wastes in rusty old drums and concrete caissons
cramming biological uglies into old trains
that run on undetermined schedules
across the landscape
and somewhere, sunken tanks of arsenic
are cloaked in barnacles
and rust slowly in salt water
and now and then, on october afternoons
underground explosions occur
and smiling spokesmen describe them as necessary and safe
while desert floors collapse
and islands tremble
and the smiling spokesman says
the san andreas fault
remains faultless
and it is the morning and the evening of the fifth day
and the seagulls are dying

on the sixth day,
man created the additive
which differed in name, but never in purpose
and was gleefully installed in cereals and fertilizers
soft drinks and cookies
field and bug sprays
creams and cosmetics
it was added to everything man ate or drank
was added to smokestacks
and sewage
and lakes
and eventually,
even the additives had additives
and counter-antidotes to combat the counter-pollutants
and even the experts gave up explaining
exactly what the additives were to accomplish
and it was the morning and the evening of the sixth day
and the seagulls were dying ➤

on the seventh day,
there was quiet over all the earth
  except for the lapping of waves
  and the bubbling of storm drains
    and the seagulls were dying
    and the plankton
    and the oceans
    and the atmosphere
    and the trees were dying
and man
  rested

HIGHEST STANDARD OF LIVING YET

MARYA MANNES

''Three-car families'' predicted
at Chamber of Commerce meeting.

One for the Master
And one for his Mate
And one for the Monster
To pick up his Date.

Bumper to bumper,
Morning till night,
Three times as many cars
Grounded in flight.

DEAD FISH

BEVERLEY ALLINSON

dead fish
float
in
polluted lake

why don't
birds
glide
dead in smog?

SEASIDE SERENADE

OGDEN NASH

It begins when you smell a funny smell,
And it isn't vanilla or caramel,
And it isn't forget-me-nots or lilies,
Or new-mown hay, or daffy-down-dillies,
And it's not what the barber rubs on Father,
And it's awful, and yet you like it rather.
No, it's not what the barber rubs on Daddy,
It's more like an elderly finnan haddie,
Or, shall we say, an electric fan
Blowing over a sardine can.
It smells of seaweed, it smells of clams,
It's as fishy as ready-made telegrams,
It's as fishy as millions of fishy fishes,
In spite of which you find it delishes,
You could do with a second helping, please,
And that, my dears, is the ocean breeze.
And pretty soon you observe a pack
Of people reclining upon their back,
And another sight that is very common
Is people reclining upon their abdomen.
And now you lose the smell of the ocean
In the sweetish vapour of sunburn lotion,
And the sun itself seems paler and colder,
Compared to vermilion face and shoulder.
The beach is peppered with ladies who look
Like pictures out of a medical book.
Last, not least, consider the kiddies,
Chirping like crickets and Katydiddies,
Splashing, squealing, slithering, crawling,
Cheerful, tearful, boisterous, bawling,
Kiddies in clamorous crowds that swarm
Heavily over your prostrate form,
Callous kiddies who gallop in myriads
'Twist ardent Apollos and eager Nereids,
Kiddies who bring, as a priceless cup,
Something dead that a wave washed up.
Oh, I must go down to the beach, my lass,
And step on a piece of broken glass.

THE SMELL OF COLOGNE

SAMUEL TAYLOR COLERIDGE

In Köln, a town of monks and bones,
And pavements fanged with murderous stones,
And rags and hags, and hideous wenches,
I counted two and seventy stenches,
All well defined, and several stinks!
Ye nymphs that reign o'er sewers and sinks,
The river Rhine, it is well known,
Doth wash your city of Cologne;
But tell me, Nymphs, what power divine
Shall henceforth wash the river Rhine?

E. E. CUMMINGS

e
cco the uglies
t

s
ub
sub

urba
n skyline on earth between whose d
owdy

hou
se
s

l
ooms an eggyellow smear of wintry sunse
t

A PRAYER FOR NOW

IONE U. MARTHEY

There is no horizon
the lake   the sky
and the haze
merge in a dark white meringue
overflowing
with a menacing steadiness.
I close the drapes of the motel window
turn my back
but the song of the highway
defies my curtain.
The whirring dispensers of monoxide
pump their poisons
into the moisture-laden atmosphere.
Each deadly element mounts its vapour horse
compressing the living air
till infants cry
and weak hearts expire.

Lord, give us air.

QUESTION

CHRIS SAWOTIN

THIS POEM IS NOT ABOUT WHALES

JUDITH FITZGERALD

it is not about the carve
and slash of knives
it is not a lament
for ruthless bastards
thinking profit and blubber
in the same fat breath
it is not a digression
on slabs of flesh
computed in clicking brains
coming up crisp green
and competitive
nor is it about guts and entrails
sprawling across snowscapes
not about crimson rorshach shapes
in virgin white
not about the madness
of slit and sever
not about whales
not about whales

STUPIDITY STREET

RALPH HODGSON

I saw with open eyes
    Singing birds sweet
Sold in the shops
    For the people to eat,
Sold in the shops of
    Stupidity Street.

I saw in vision
    The worm in the wheat,
And in the shops nothing
    For people to eat;
Nothing for sale in
    Stupidity Street.

ONE THOUGHT EVER AT THE FORE

WALT WHITMAN

One thought ever at the fore—
That in the Divine Ship, the World, breasting Time and
    Space,
All Peoples of the globe together sail, sail the same voyage,
    are bound to the same destination.

LAUGHING DOLPHINS

MICK BURRS

Laughing dolphins cavorting in symmetry
nimble and childlike with no streak of mean
while it is men who look down
to transform the clowns
into something more human, less aquamarine.

We are superior we sincerely believe
training the dolphin in ways to deceive
though each giver of glee
might happen to be
wiser than you and kinder than me.

I think I will try to learn what I can
from creatures less destructive than man
and make of my earth
what they make of their sea
a playground for mirth, for harmony.

CREDO

ROBERT FULGHUM

All I really need to know
about how to live and what to do and how to be
I learned in kindergarten.
Wisdom was not at the top of the graduate-school mountain,
but there in the sandpile at Sunday School.
These are the things I learned:

Share everything.
Play fair.
Don't hit people.
Put things back where you found them.
Clean up your own mess.
Don't take things that aren't yours.
Say you're sorry when you hurt somebody.
Wash your hands before you eat.
Flush.
Warm cookies and cold milk are good for you.
Live a balanced life—
learn some and think some
and draw and paint and sing and dance and play
and work every day some.

Take a nap every afternoon.
When you go out into the world,
watch out for traffic,
hold hands,
and stick together.

Be aware of wonder.
Remember the little seed in the Styrofoam cup:
The roots go down and the plant goes up
and nobody really knows how or why,
but we are all like that.
Goldfish and hamsters and white mice
and even the little seed in the Styrofoam cup—they all die.
So do we.

And then remember the Dick-and-Jane books
and the first word you learned—
the biggest word of all—LOOK.

Everything you need to know is in there somewhere.
The Golden Rule and love and basic sanitation.
Ecology and politics and equality and sane living.

Think what a better world it would be if
we all—the whole world—
had cookies and milk about three o'clock every afternoon
and then lay down with our blankies for a nap.
Or if all governments had as a basic policy
to always put things back where they found them
and to clean up their own mess.

And it is still true,
no matter how old you are—
when you go out into the world,
it is best to hold hands and stick together.

from DESIDERATA

MAX EHRMANN

You are a child of the universe,
no less than the trees and the stars:
you have a right to be here.
And whether or not it is clear to you,
no doubt the universe is unfolding as it should.
Therefore be at peace with God,
    whatever you conceive him to be;
and whatever your labour and aspirations,
in the noisy confusion of life
keep peace within your soul.
With all its shams, drudgery and broken dreams,
it is still a beautiful world.
    Strive to be happy.

LET US REBUILD

W.W.E. ROSS
(translated from the French of Max Jacob)

It is enough that a child of five, in pale blue blouse, should draw pictures in an album for a door to open into the light, for the castle to be rebuilt, and the dry brown of the hillside to be covered with flowers.

from THE PASTURE

ROBERT FROST

I'm going out to clean the pasture spring;
I'll only stop to rake the leaves away
(And wait to watch the water clear, I may):
I sha'n't be gone long.—You come too.

Seven Days/*Gary Dunford/p. 192*
This poem was first published in 1971. Since that time, we have identified many other environmentally destructive behaviours that occur daily.

Write a different "sixth day" verse for this poem. Choose an issue that has recently been in the public eye and conscience. Imitate Dunford's style but consider the fact that nowadays we tend to avoid whenever possible the use of "man" when referring to humanity.

Dead Fish/*Beverley Allinson/p. 194*
Write a short poem which deals with how a particular aspect of nature is being affected by pollution. Find or create an illustration to accompany your poem.

this poem is not about whales/*Judith Fitzgerald/p. 198*
Research the topic of whale hunting. When you have completed your research and have decided what your views on the subject are, write a letter to the editor of your local newspaper explaining your opinions.

Mail your letter. Do not be surprised if it appears in print!

Credo/*Robert Fulghum/p. 200*
According to Fulghum, everything he needs to know, he learned in kindergarten. Where did you learn everything you need to know? Write your own statement of beliefs, outlining the things that you have learned. Choose a location other than a kindergarten class from which to draw your observations. What might you learn, for example, from a playground, a garden, a forest, a football field, or a dance floor? Try to relate at least some of your observations to the environmental theme.

Let Us Rebuild/*W.W.E. Ross/p. 202*
Ross believes that there are reasons enough to rebuild our dreams and hopes for the future. Do you agree?

Write a poem or paragraph expressing your views on the importance of taking the first steps towards reclaiming a dying planet.

THE GREATER PERSPECTIVE

1. During a recent holiday, you revisited an area that you remember as having been forested with large, old trees. This time there were only stumps. You have seen first-hand the effects of the "clear-cutting" practices of a local pulp or lumber mill.
   Write one letter to the president of the lumber company and another to the editor of your local newspaper, expressing how you feel about such practices. You might wish to mail the letter to the editor. Do not be surprised if it is printed in the newspaper.
2. Create a concrete poem dealing with an environmental issue of particular concern to you. Remember that the look of your poem should suggest its meaning or purpose.
3. In groups, conduct a research project to determine how "environmentally aware" a particular industry or business in your community is. Prepare a report to be presented to the class. Invite civil officials and/or representatives from the companies researched to hear your presentation and to speak to the class. You might also wish to present "certificates of appreciation" to the more environmentally conscious organizations identified.

12 HERE COMES THE SUN

Give me the splendid silent sun with all its beams full-dazzling,
Give me juicy autumnal fruit ripe and red from the orchard,
Give me a field where the unmow'd grass grows. . .
Give me a garden of beautiful flowers where I can walk undisturb'd.

WALT WHITMAN

RENEWAL

Most of us learn very quickly that the only constant in life is change. As we grow older, we find that our lives, our values and our attitudes are continually changing. Sometimes these changes, when viewed from a perspective of distance and time, can be seen as falling into patterns or cycles.

The first series of poems in this chapter suggests that with each new day and spring, there is a renewal not only in the world of nature but also in our own lives.

Lynne Ferguson, in her poem, ''To the Friend I Broke Up With'' (page 92) suggests that ''Life is a jigsaw puzzle/And people are the little pieces.'' There are times during the process of piecing the puzzle together that we wonder if the effort is worthwhile. Fortunately, most of us do succeed in putting the pieces together and coming to terms with that puzzle called life.

The process of renewal and reaffirmation may be long and painful but the rewards are well worth it.

What delights me in the spring is more a sensation than an appearance, more a hope than a visible reality. There is something in the softness of the air, in the beginning of the days, in the very sounds and odours of the time that caresses us and consoles us after the rigours of winter.

T.G. HAMERTON

There is no time like the Spring
When life's alive in everything.

CHRISTINA ROSSETTI

What humbugs we are who pretend to live for Beauty, and never see the Dawn!

LOGAN PEARSALL SMITH

Like an army defeated
The snow hath retreated.

WILLIAM WORDSWORTH

THE DAWN; THE BIRDS'

W.W.E. ROSS

The dawn; the birds'
tumultuous clamour
grows as the light
gradually
makes more distinct
the rocks, the trees.
picking out each
from among the grey.

The clamour grows
and noises mingle—
of water slapping
along the rocks—
all the sounds
of the dawn, the early
morning, all
the early sounds.

And more distinct
the rocks, the trees,
and brighter now
the early lighting—
when suddenly
all these sounds cease—
a strange silence
and then the sun!

ALBA

DEREK WALCOTT

Dawn breaking as I woke,
With the white sweat of the dew
On the green, new grass
I walked in the cold, quiet as
If it were the world beginning;
Peeling and eating a chilled tangerine.
I may have many sorrows,
Dawn is not one of them

SPRING

WALT WHITMAN

I said in my heart, ''I am sick of four walls and a ceiling
I have need of the sky.
I have business with the grass.
I will up and get me away where the hawk is wheeling,
Lone and high,
And the slow clouds go by . . .''

Here Comes the Sun

GEORGE HARRISON

Here comes the sun. Here comes the sun
and I say . . . It's alright

Little darling, it's been a long cold lonely winter
Little darling it feels like years since it's been here
Here comes the sun. Here comes the sun
and I say . . . It's alright

Little darling, the smile's returning to their faces
Little darling, it seems like years since it's been here
Here comes the sun. Here comes the sun and I say
It's alright

Sun, sun, sun, here it comes
Sun, sun, sun, here it comes
Sun, sun, sun, here it comes
Sun, sun, sun, here it comes

Little darling, I feel the ice is slowly melting
Little darling it seems like years since it's been clear
Here comes the sun. Here comes the sun
and I say . . . It's alright

Here comes the sun
Here comes the sun
It's alright

True Enjoyment

AUTHOR UNKNOWN

I drink tea on the terrace at sunset all alone.
Spring breezes fan me as I moisten my brush on stone.
Sitting in perfect comfort, I write a poem on a palm.
A kingfisher chirps on a bamboo clothes-rack safe from harm;
A dragonfly clings to a fishing line, buzzing his warm refrain.
Now that I know what enjoyment is,
I'll come here again and again!

May All Earth Be Clothed in Light

GEORGE HITCHCOCK

Morning spreads over
the beaches like lava;
the waves lie still, they
glitter with pieces of light.

I stand at the window
& watch a heron on one leg,
its plumage white in the green banks
of mint. Behind me
smoke rises from a nest
of bricks, the brass clock
on the kitchen shelf
judges & spares.

Slowly the bird
opens its dazzling wings.
I am filled with joy.
The fields are awake!
the fields with their hidden lizards
& fire of new iris.

Warm Rain

MIDORI IWASAKI

Warm
rain
runs
off fresh green boughs
and
wets
my cheek

as I sail out
into
a
new
morning

Metaphor

EVE MERRIAM

Morning is
a new sheet of paper
for you to write on.

Whatever you want to say,
all day,
until night
folds it up
and files it away.

The bright words and the dark words
are gone
until dawn
and a new day
to write on.

Return

DAVID HELWIG

After the white nights
of solitaire
within the prison of the winter heart,
only the dead
can speak of less than daffodils
or singing birds,
bright feathered birds.

But the first to return
are crows,
black scavengers
strutting awkwardly over the spring earth.

Only black birds
that live close to death
can come here.

But strident as they are
we must love them
just for their speaking of rebirth.

February

NELSON BALL

I wonder about
the worms & the ants—

will they ever
come alive again?

MARCH AFTERNOON

ELIZABETH BREWSTER

Suddenly it is spring
and cars come splashing
rivers of mud and water
while people walking leap
over rippling puddles,
balance on ice and slime.

Brown snow melts,
mixed with candy wrappers,
last year's leaves,
cigarette butts
and crushed red berries,

and overhead the sky
softens
is a paler blue
tepid
where one cloud floats.

Coats are unbuttoned,
scarves thrust into pockets,
and there—one girl who abandoned
rubber boots too early
picks her way delicately
over the small islands of mud
and ice.

TREE PLANTING

ENDRE FARKAS

It's about roots

matted, pulpy, delicate
lying sideways on the lawn
wrapped in temporary earth

It's about rituals

the spade & I & you
incising a holy circle

It's about digging holes

It's about right

It's about reunion

earth's black wormy love
embracing the myriad of mouths
along which the seasons' juices flow

It's about supports

It's about family

It's about stepping back
and making a silent blessing
over something that is clean

It's about washing up,
entwining

It's about flowering

from SPRING WATERS

PING HSIN
(translated by Kenneth Rexroth and Ling Chung)

The commonplace puddle
Reflects the setting sun
And becomes the Sea of Gold.

Fueled

MARCIE HANS

Fueled
by a million
man-made
wings of fire—
the rocket tore a tunnel
through the sky—
and everybody cheered.
Fueled
only by a thought from God—
the seedling
urged its way
through the thickness of black—
and as it pierced
the heavy ceiling of the soil—
and launched itself
up into outer space—
no
one
even
clapped.

Bonsai, Haiku, a Seashell

ELIZABETH GOURLAY

I have seen a tree
ten inches tall resplendent
with tiny blue plums

I have read a poem
seventeen sounds redolent
of jasmine and love

once in mid-winter
I was offered a present
small brown and white shell

mollusk in water
most magically rent
grew into a flower

dear sloe-eyed artists
let me state this   there can be
no phoenix too frequent

I Meant to Do My Work Today

RICHARD LeGALLIENNE

I meant to do my work today—
  But a brown bird sang in the apple-tree,
And a butterfly flitted across the field,
  And all the leaves were calling me.

And the wind went sighing over the land,
  Tossing the grasses to and fro,
And a rainbow held out its shining hand—
  So what could I do but laugh and go?

SPRING'S MIRACLE

PHYLLIS DAVIES

Spring rejuvenates.

Our perception shifts.
That's a miracle.

Spring focusses on the *now*.

Flowers,
leaves,
the songs of birds
all burst forth
with the joy of this moment.

Spring sings, ''Remember.''

''Look,
feel,
remember.
Memories are part
of who we are today.''

Spring eloquently touches me.

It helps me
reach out in love,
even when I'm hurting.
Sharing love and caring
softens my pain,
brings joy
and courage to others.

Spring gives life to what looked dead.

Life was there
though unseen
in leafless
trees.

Spring brings a timeless cycle of renewal.

It lets me know
that life goes on
for those we love
but cannot see.

THIS FEVERS ME

RICHARD EBERHART

This fevers me, this sun on green,
On grass glowing, this young spring.
The secret hallowing is come,
Regenerate sudden incarnation,
Mystery made visible
In growth, yet subtly veiled in all,
Ununderstandable in grass,
In flowers, and in the human heart,
This lyric mortal loveliness,
The earth breathing, and the sun.
The young lambs sport, none udderless.
Rabbits dash beneath the brush.
Crocuses have come; wind flowers
Tremble against quick April.
Violets put on the night's blue,
Primroses wear the pale dawn,
The gold daffodils have stolen
From the sun. New grass leaps up;
Gorse yellows, starred with day;
The willow is a graceful dancer
Poised; the poplar poises too.
The apple takes the seafoam's light,
And the evergreen tree is densely bright.
April, April, when will he
Be gaunt, be old, who is so young?
This fevers me, this sun on green,
On grass glowing, this young spring.

A DARK THING INSIDE THE DAY

LINDA GREGG

So many want to be lifted by song and dancing,
and this morning it is easy to understand.
I write in the sound of chirping birds hidden
in the almond trees, the almonds still green

and thriving in the foliage. Up the street,
a man is hammering to make a new house as doves
continue their low cooing forever. Bees humming
and high above that a brilliant clear sky.
The roses are blooming and I smell the sweetness.
Everything desirable is here already in abundance.
And the sea. The dark thing is hardly visible
in the leaves, under the sheen. We sleep easily.
So I bring no sad stories to warn the heart.
All the flowers are adult this year. The good
world gives and the white doves praise all of it.

THE HEALING

from The Beautyway Chant
NAVAJO TRADITIONAL

All the things that have harmed me,
  they will leave me.
I walk with a cool body after they leave me.
Inside of me today I will be well,
  all fever will have come out of me,
  and go away from me,
  and leave my head cool.
I will hear today
I will see today
I will be in my right mind today.
Today I will walk out
Today everything evil will leave me
  I will be as I was before
  I will have a cool breeze over my body
  I will walk with a light body.
I will be happy forever,
  nothing will hinder me,
I will walk with Beauty before me.
I will walk with Beauty behind me.
I will walk with Beauty above me.
I will walk with Beauty below me.
I will walk with Beauty all around me
I will walk and speak Beautiful words.
I will forever be one,
Everything is Beautiful.

POEM FOR MY FATHER

GWEN FITZHUGH

Knees bend
Onto the moist earth
Fresh from plowing.
Eyes close,
Savouring the richness
As a young woman
Savours the kiss of her beloved.
You smile conspiratorily
At the young daughter
Watching, unsure.
''Have you ever smelled the earth?
Doesn't it smell *good*?''
From the offered hands
Cupped tightly,
The little girl
Sniffs the rich blackness
And knows
She shares a special secret.

Years pass.
I pause,
Reflect,
And know
Where I learned poetry.

The Dawn; The Birds'/*W.W.E. Ross/p. 207*
There are many possible different ways of looking at sunrises and morning. It all depends on one's perspective. Write a paragraph or poem that describes the approach of morning as seen through the eyes of one of the following:

a) a young child or teenager on a school day;
b) an older person who has lived a long life;
c) a young person who is trying to deal with the recent death of a loved one;
d) a dreamer;
e) a doer;
f) an idealist;
g) a cynic or pessimist;
h) someone in love;
i) someone who has been hurt by love.

Here Comes the Sun/*George Harrison/p. 208*
Write a letter to George Harrison or to your favourite rock performer/group in which you explain what it is you like about a particular song or album. You might wish to express gratitude to the performer(s) for the benefits you have received from the music. Be specific in terms of songs or album titles and the effect(s) they have on you.

Metaphor/*Eve Merriam/p. 210*
Develop your own metaphor for the morning. Choose some common object for your extended comparison. You may imitate Merriam's poem if you wish.

March Afternoon/*Elizabeth Brewster/p. 211*
The speaker in this poem has focussed on the less pleasant features of early spring.

Imagine that you are the speaker and that you have met a close friend on the street. Write a dialogue in which you complain to your friend about spring and in which your friend responds by emphasizing the many positive characteristics of the season.

I Meant To Do My Work Today/*Richard LeGallienne/p. 212*
Imagine you are the employer of the speaker in this poem. He has just offered you his excuse for missing work the previous day. Write your response to him. You might wish to do so in prose or you might choose to create a parody of the LeGallienne poem.

The Healing from The Beautyway Chant/*Navajo Traditional/p. 215*
Either

a) Prepare and tape record a reading of this selection using appropriate background music;

or

b) Create an illustrated poster of the selection.

THE GREATER PERSPECTIVE

1. In 1915, the poet Julian Grenfell wrote: ''And life is colour and warmth and light/ And a striving evermore for these.'' Nearly eighty years have passed since then and many features of our world, as well as many of our perspectives of life have changed. How would you describe life? Select a format (poem, newspaper report, short story, radio broadcast, television commercial, etc.) and write your views on ''And life is . . . ''

2. Have you ever said ''thank you'' to any of the people who have helped you become what you are today? Select someone who has had a major influence in your life (a parent, guardian, other relative, teacher, friend, etc.) and write a letter or a dialogue in which you thank this person for helping you achieve the perspectives you now have.

GLOSSARY

ALLEGORIES are short narratives involving simple plots and characters; their purpose is to teach moral lessons. They work on two different levels: the surface or *literal level of meaning* usually involves simple characters and basic plots that are appealing and easy to follow. However, to be fully appreciated, a second, more important level of meaning, the *symbolic level*, must be considered. Here the reader finds that each element in the allegory has a symbolic equivalent in the real world. The moral lessons with which most allegories conclude are obvious and logical extensions of the story.

In Stephen Crane's ''Many Workmen'' (p. 129), for example, the plot is simple but improbable; the characters are basic and undeveloped. On the surface level of meaning, the poem can be dismissed as being too unrealistic to be worthy of discussion. However, if we can come to terms with what the workmen represent, what the ball they are building symbolizes, the significance of building it on the mountain-top, the role the workmen's pride and comments play in their fate, and what moral message can be derived from that fate, the story in the poem takes on a whole new meaning and importance.

ALLITERATION involves the repetition of similar or identical sounds found in the beginning of two or more words. It is a popular poetic device that finds its way into many media. Newspaper headlines, movie and TV program titles, names of rock bands, sports teams, entertainment personalities, song titles, and even consumer products frequently use alliteration. Alliteration depends on sound and not spelling. In ''First Person Demonstrative,'' (p. 89), for example, ''I'd rather *wr*ench'' is an example of this musical device despite the difference in the initial letter of each word.

ALLUSION is a brief reference to a person, event or thing that the writer assumes the reader will recognize. Such references may come from history, current events, the Bible, mythology, or literature. Allusions occur in many forms of communication including everyday conversation. If you refer to a person as being an ''Attila the Hun,'' it is quite obvious to your listener precisely what you mean. Notice the economy of words possible with allusion —only three words are necessary to convey information not only about the characteristics of the person, but also about your attitude towards him or her. Movies, novels, TV shows, short fiction, and advertisements are all rich sources of and for allusions.

AMBIGUITY is that quality in language and words which makes possible more than one interpretation of a work.

ANALOGY is a process in which a complex idea is compared to a simple, or more familiar, idea. (''Love Is,'' p. 85)

APOSTROPHE is an impassioned address to something abstract (e.g., youth, love, death), to someone absent as if he or she were present, to something inanimate (e.g., sea, wind, tree), or to someone dead as if he or she could respond. This technique is often used to express powerful emotions. (''To Youth,'' p. 37; ''Apostrophe to Man,'' p. 140)

ASSONANCE is the repetition of stressed vowel sounds as in: thr*ee*/b*ea*ch; s*ay*/pl*ay*ed; fl*a*me/p*ai*n.

BLANK VERSE is a form of poetry which does not depend on rhyme for its rhythm. It is usually written in iambic pentameter. Most of Shakespeare's plays are written in blank verse.

CACOPHONY occurs when the poet uses unpleasant sounding words or rhythms to create a jarring effect. Its opposite is *euphony*.

CONCRETE POETRY is a form of poetry in which the shape and pattern of a poem suggests its meaning and purpose. (''The Philosophers,'' p. 19; ''Deforestation,'' p. 187)

CONNOTATION *see Denotation*.

CONSONANCE involves the repetition of final consonant sounds in a series of words. For example: stru*ts* and fre*ts*; fir*st* and la*st*.

CONTRAST is often used by writers to define or clarify a certain idea or value judgment. Contrasting one element with another serves to highlight their respective differences, and thereby brings both into a clearer focus than would have been possible if they were dealt with separately.

DENOTATION is the literal, dictionary meaning of a word. *Connotation*, however, refers to the many different associated meanings and suggestions that individual readers have for a particular word. For example, coming to terms with the denotation of the word ''house'' is a relatively simple matter since it means basically the same thing to most people. Coming to terms with the connotations of the word ''home'' is more difficult. Some readers might associate ''home'' with such things as warmth, family, love, and security. Others might have quite different emotional associations with the same word. Poems derive their richness of meaning through the connotative power of words.

DICTION refers to the author's choice of words and phrases in a work. The diction of a poem may be described in many different ways, such as simple, sophisticated, colloquial, formal or informal.

DIDACTIC VERSE is a term used to describe poems which seem to preach or moralize. In such works, a ''proper'' mode of conduct or behaviour is presented directly, in a deliberate attempt to change the reader's attitude or behaviour. In other words, the lesson being taught is more important to the writer than the artistic qualities of the work. This is why the word ''didactic'' is often used as a derogatory term in the discussion of literature. Determining the degree to which a poem is didactic is usually a matter of opinion. What may appear didactic to one person may not necessarily be so to another.

DRAMATIC MONOLOGUE refers to a type of poem which projects the conversation of one person to a silent, but identifiable audience. There is also a specific physical setting and dramatic situation to which the speaker is responding. Dramatic monologues are similar to the soliloquy in effect. The purpose of both is to enable readers to learn more about the speaker's thoughts and feelings. (''Lament,'' p.108)

ELEGY is a serious poem, the purpose of which is to express grief or sorrow. The theme is always a serious one, usually death.

EPIGRAM is a brief, pithy statement. An epigram usually consists of two rhyming lines and makes a statement that is witty and memorable. Epigrams (unrhyming) appear in prose as well as poetry: ''Prose is the kind of writing everybody understands, poetry is the other kind.'' (Louis Dudek)

EUPHEMISM refers to the usage of inoffensive or neutral words in the place of harsher, more realistic words. Euphemisms are often used to reduce the risk of offending or upsetting people who are in vulnerable or painful situations. If someone has died, for example, we might describe that person as having ''passed away.'' Euphemisms are also used when dealing with subjects of a personal nature such as birth, death, funeral arrangements, bodily functions, success and failure.

EUPHONY is the musical effect achieved when a poet uses words and phrases that create pleasant, harmonious sounds and rhythms. The opposite of *cacophony*.

FOOT refers to the basic unit of rhythm found within a line of verse. A metrical foot usually consists of one accented syllable and one or two unaccented syllables. There are many different kinds of metrical feet: the *iamb* consists of one unaccented syllable and one accented syllable (''trapeze''); the *trochee* has one accented and one unaccented syllable (''major''); the *dactyl* consists of one accented syllable followed by two unaccented ones (''following''); and the *spondee* is characterized by its two accented syllables (''spondee'').

FOUND POETRY is exactly that. Have you ever read a piece of prose, or a cake mix box, and felt that what you were reading was rather poetic? This is a common experience for many readers. Some writers have taken this feeling further, and have actually made a living from collecting snatches of poetic prose from unlikely places (such as history books, cereal boxes, news stories, board-game rules, or death certificates), arranging them on the page so that they look like poetry, and then publishing the results as found poetry. John Robert Colombo's *John Toronto*, for example, is made up entirely of found poems taken from the prose writings of John Strachan, the first Bishop of Toronto; *Mostly Monsters* consists of found poems taken from the dialogue of Hollywood monster movies. (*from* ''The Diary of a Young Girl,'' p. 132)

FREE VERSE is poetry which contains no structured form or rhyme scheme, and does not follow a standard metrical pattern. Free verse is as old as the 1611, King James' Version of the Bible.

The initial response to free verse was less than favourable and few poets used it till Walt Whitman popularized the form in the 1850s. It then quickly came to be recognized as being not only acceptable but also, in many cases, the preferred form of poetic expression.

The voice used in modern free verse is close to a natural speaking voice. As a result, many readers are attracted to free verse poems because they are "easier to understand." However, there are other readers who are unable to accept free verse as "poetry." Poetry, they argue, should have structure and perhaps even rhyme, and they find it difficult to distinguish between free verse and poetic prose. ("I Feel (Vers Libre)," p. 6)

HAIKU is a popular form of verse developed by the Japanese during the 17th century. It traditionally consists of three lines, containing respectively 5, 7 and 5 syllables. Haiku usually offers an implied comment, thought or feeling by presenting either a description of nature or two images which contrast with each other. Today, writers do not always adhere to the original form or tradition, and the number of syllables per line may vary.

HYPERBOLE is deliberate exaggeration in order to emphasize a fact or a feeling. It can be used to create either a comic or serious effect but, in spite of the exaggeration, there is nearly always some truth expressed in the hyperbole.

IAMBIC PENTAMETER is the metre most frequently used in Shakespeare's plays and sonnets. *Iambic* refers to the metrical foot consisting of an unstressed and stressed syllable; pentameter refers to the presence of five (penta) feet within the line. A line of iambic pentameter will, therefore, contain ten syllables. For example: "Once more/unto/the breach,/dear friends,/once more;" ("Once More Unto the Breach," p. 141)

IMAGERY is the technique by which a writer appeals to sensory experience through description. To communicate effectively, poets must refer to those sensory experiences which most readers have in common.

Images may be taken literally and simply if the description is a direct representation of a common sensory experience such as green grass, dark shadow, the smell of cedar, the stench of smoke, the buzz of a power saw, wet sand squeezed between toes, and the sweet stickiness of honey. The poet who uses such descriptions cannot help but strike a common chord with the reader. Images that cannot be taken literally, but force the reader to use his or her imagination to make a connection, are figurative devices. These can be more specifically identified as metaphors, similes or personification.

IRONY refers to a situation or to a usage of words in which there is a discrepancy between expectation and actuality. For example, we would expect a pilot to be in control of the aircraft and know its ultimate destination; it would be ironic if he or she became lost and transported us to the wrong airport. We might consider it ironic if a forest is destroyed to produce paper that will be used to criticize the destruction of forests. In these cases, what actually occurs is inconsistent with what we expect, and we cannot help but laugh wryly at the turn of events.

Poets use irony frequently for specific purposes such as emphasizing a theme, or reminding us that life is not always as simple as it seems.

JUXTAPOSITION involves the combining of improbable elements in close proximity to each other. Its effectiveness comes from the shock created by the combination. For example, in the third verse of Edwin Brock's "Five Ways to Kill a Man" (p. 145), the juxtaposition of the "plague of rats" and the "dozen songs" is striking and memorable for the cynical perspective it projects.

LITOTES *see Understatement.*

LYRIC is a short poem which expresses a powerful emotion or sentiment.

LYRICS are the words of a song.

MEIOSIS *see Understatement.*

METAPHOR involves a comparison between two essentially unlike elements. "This classroom is a zoo" is a metaphor since classrooms and zoos are quite different, and yet sometimes there are bases for comparisons. If the comparison is extended by developing further points of similarity, an *extended metaphor* results.

METONYMY involves using a closely related object to represent another object. *Synecdoche* occurs when a part or significant feature of an object is used to stand for or represent the whole object. It is often difficult to differentiate between these two figures of speech and therefore we are increasingly using *metonymy* to refer to both instances.

We use metonymy frequently in everyday conversations. We drive "wheels," not cars, we are always ready to lend the teacher an "ear," and to give performers a "hand" for entertaining us.

When the speaker in "Tears Are Not Enough," (p. 176) suggests that we lend a "hand," it is not literally intended that we should cut off one of our hands. What is meant is that the whole person should lend assistance. "Tears" are also a metonymous reference in that they represent but a small part of the total idea of showing sympathy and compassion.

MOOD is the dominant feeling or atmosphere of a work, created through the author's choice of words and details.

OCTAVE refers to the first eight lines of a Petrarchan sonnet. *See Sonnet.*

ODE is a form of lyric poetry characterized by its exalted, elaborate vocabulary and tone. It usually focusses on a single, serious subject which it treats in an emotionally charged intellectual manner.

Odes (*Pindaric* and *Horatian*) are highly structured in form. However, a third type of ode (*irregular*) is much freer in form. Wordsworth's "Intimations of Immortality" (p. 24) is an example of this latter type. The line lengths and stanza forms in it vary, and the poem follows no fixed pattern. The elevated or exalted tone is, nevertheless, maintained by the use of the iambic metre.

ONOMATOPOEIA is a figure of speech in which a word used closely resembles the sound to which it refers. Our language is rich with onomatopoeic words such as hiss, knock, slap, buzz, fizz, snarl, whirr and splash. These words, because they are so recognizably close to the sound being described, can be used with subtle effect to enhance meaning and tone.

OXYMORON involves a combination of two contradictory or conflicting words. An oxymoron is different from a *paradox* in that it compactly creates its effect through the combination of two successive words, while a paradox involves a complete statement. For example: jumbo shrimp, pretty ugly, eloquent silence, wise fool.

PARADOX is a statement that reads as being contradictory but upon closer examination reveals some truth. For example: ''I lived in poverty/And died rich.'' (''On the Way to School,'' p. 55)

PARODY is a comical or satirical imitation of a well- known work. The purpose of a parody might simply be to ridicule the style of the original, or it might be to criticize and satirize the ideas presented in it. The following is a parody of Herrick's ''Gather Ye Rose-buds'' (p. 68):

Gather Kitten while you may,
  Time brings only Sorrow;
  And the Kittens of To-day
Will be Old Cats Tomorrow.
    —Oliver Herford (1863–1935)

PATHETIC FALLACY is the false belief (fallacy) that nature mirrors what is going on in the lives, minds or hearts of people. This device is frequently used in books, poems and movies. Lovers, for example, are often depicted as meeting on warm spring days, but breaking up on cold winter nights. Murder or heinous crimes are usually described as being planned or perpetrated on dark and stormy evenings. (''Memory from Childhood,'' p. 48)

PERSONIFICATION is a specialized form of *metaphor* in which human characteristics are attributed to things or ideas. Effective use of personification stimulates our imagination and increases our understanding of whatever has been given human qualities. It makes the abstract more concrete by reducing it to familiar human forms and behaviour.

QUATRAIN is a stanza containing four lines.

REPETITION of words, phrases and sounds is used in poetry to create rhythm or emphasis.

RHYME can occur in various forms, and it is sometimes important in our analysis of poetry to consider the kinds of rhymes used by the poet. A careful consideration of the nature and frequency of rhymes can help the reader to a better appreciation of the tone and purpose of the work. Rhymes create rhythm, and rhythm projects emotion and attitude.

To determine the kind of rhyme being used, count the number of syllables that sound similar. If only the last syllable rhymes, we have a *single rhyme* (also referred to as masculine rhyme). For example: crime/grime, resent/content. If two syllables rhyme, then it is a *double rhyme* (also referred to as feminine rhyme). For example: resenting/contenting, myrtle/fertile. If three syllables rhyme, this is a *triple rhyme*. For example: pollution/solution, laborious/victorious.

Rhymes are also classified in terms of where they appear in the line. The most common type, *end rhyme*, occurs at the end of the line. *Internal rhyme* occurs when a word within the line rhymes with another word within the same line.

SATIRE is a form of literature that ridicules some aspect of human behaviour, customs or attitudes in an attempt to bring about a positive change. Unlike comedians, satirists do not believe in humour for its own sake, but rather see it as a means to an end. They believe that one way to effect change is to get people to laugh at themselves since by laughing at ourselves, and the things we do, we take ourselves less seriously. Sometimes this alone is enough to commence the process of change. ("The Walrus and the Carpenter," p. 188; "Five Ways to Kill a Man," p. 145)

SIMILE is a comparison between two essentially unlike things using the words "like" or "as." Not many people agree with Dogberry in Shakespeare's *Much Ado About Nothing* when he says that ". . . comparisons are odorous." We often use analogies and evocative similes to clarify thoughts, explain complex ideas, advertise products and generally make our writing more colourful and appealing.

SONNET is a fourteen line lyric poem. (There are four different sonnet forms but for purposes of this anthology we will consider only the two major ones most commonly found.)

The sonnet was first developed in Italy during the thirteenth century and brought to its height of perfection in the following century by Petrarch. In the early sixteenth century, Thomas Wyatt, a translator of Petrarch's sonnets, altered the form and developed the English Sonnet. Because Shakespeare wrote the most highly respected poems using this variation, his name is often used to describe this form of sonnet.

The *Italian* or *Petrarchan* sonnet consists of an octave with a rhyme scheme *abbaabba* and a sestet whose rhyme scheme is either *cdecde, cdedce* or *cdccdc*. The octave generally presents a situation, or position on a theme, or raises a question on a particular issue. The sestet responds to this, perhaps offering a comment or observation on the idea presented in the octave, or suggesting an answer to the question posed.

The *English* or *Shakespearean* sonnet is divided into four distinct parts: three quatrains and a concluding rhyming couplet. The rhyme scheme is usually *abab cdcd efef gg*. Normally, the three quatrains offer three separate examples of, or statements on, a theme. The couplet suggests a conclusion or final statement that is often epigrammatic and provides a climactic finish to the sonnet.

SOUND AND SENSE Alexander Pope (1688–1744) wrote that ''the sound [in a poem] must seem an echo to the sense.'' This can be accomplished in a number of ways. One of the most effective methods of conveying meaning through sound is by the use of long and short vowels. Words and lines that contain long vowels create a monotonous, melancholic atmosphere. Similarly, words and lines that contain short, quick vowels create a lively skipping beat that translates into a more energetic message.

If you read ''Bird in the Classroom,'' (p. 56) aloud, paying careful attention to the length of the lines and exaggerating the long and short vowels, you will notice how the first two verses contrast in sound sense, with the verses which describe the cheerful song of the bird.

SYMBOLISM is the use of a concrete object to represent an abstract idea or concept. Many symbols have become so much a part of our cultural traditions that they are immediately identifiable. (A red rose/love; a dove/peace; a hawk/war; a black cat/bad luck; a rabbit's foot/good luck)

SYNECDOCHE *see Metonymy.*

TONE refers to the author's attitude towards the subject.

UNDERSTATEMENT occurs when we say less than what we actually mean, or use less force than the context requires. We hope that our audience will make up the difference through the workings of their imaginations.

Understatement comes in a variety of forms. When an opinion is offered by stating the negative of what is actually intended, this is known as *litotes.* ''Elvis is not a bad singer,'' is litotes when said by an Elvis fan. *Meiosis* is a deliberate understatement that is used for the sake of emphasis, or to create a humorous effect. If you notice a three block line-up for a popular movie and you say, ''What a nice little line-up,'' you are using meiosis.

INDEX OF AUTHORS

INDEX OF TITLES

Acknowledgments

Every effort has been made to trace the ownership of all copyright material and to secure the necessary permissions to reprint the selections. In the event of any question arising as to the use of any of the material, the editor and the publisher, while expressing regret for any inadvertent error, will be happy to make the necessary correction in future printings.

The editor and the publisher make grateful acknowledgments for permission to reprint the following copyright material. Acknowledgments are made by author in alphabetical order.

"Be Quiet, Stand Still" by Virginia C. Abbott reprinted with permission of the author.

"Dead Fish" by Beverley Allinson from *Space Poems* (Nelson, 1972) reprinted with permission of the author.

"Paradise" by Cecilia E. Alonso reprinted with permission of the author.

"Poeti-c Art" by Arudra reprinted with permission of the Asian Studies Center, Michigan State University.

"Success Story" by Margaret Atwood reprinted with permission of the Canadian Publishers, McClelland & Stewart, Toronto. "It Is Dangerous to Read Newspapers" by Margaret Atwood from *Selected Poems 1966-1984*, © Margaret Atwood, 1990, reprinted with permission of Oxford University Press Canada.

"Musée des Beaux Arts" from *W.H. Auden: Collected Poems*, ed. Edward Mendelson. Copyright © 1976 by Edward Mendelson, William Meredith, and Monroe K. Spears, Executors of the Estate of W.H. Auden. Reprinted by permission of Random House, Inc.

"A Song of Greatness" from *The Children Sing in the Far West* by Mary Austin. Copyright 1928 by Mary Austin. Copyright © renewed 1956 by Kenneth M. Chapman and Mary C. Wheelwright. Reprinted by permission of Houghton Mifflin Co.

"Educator" by Shelly Barge from *English Journal* (October 1985). Copyright 1985 by the National Council of Teachers of English. Reprinted with permission.

"The Peace of Wild Things" from *Openings*, copyright © 1968 by Wendell Berry, reprinted by permission of Harcourt Brace Jovanovich, Inc.

"World War III" from *The Collected Poems of Earle Birney* by Earle Birney. Used by permission of the Canadian Publishers, McClelland & Stewart, Toronto.

"A Poem for High School Anthologies" by George Bowering from *Another Mouth* (McClelland & Stewart, 1979). Reprinted with permission of the author.

"Slow Guitar" © Edward Kamau Brathwaite 1973. Reprinted from *The Arrivants* by Edward Kamau Brathwaite (1973) by permission of Oxford University Press.

"Mirrors" by Elizabeth Brewster is reprinted from *Selected Poems* by permission of Oberon Press. "On the Value of Fantasies" by Elizabeth Brewster is reprinted from *Sometimes I Think of Moving* by permission of Oberon Press. "March Afternoon" by Elizabeth Brewster is reprinted from *Sunrise North* by permission of Oberon Press.

"Five Ways to Kill a Man" by Edwin Brock from *Invisibility Is the Art of Survival*. Copyright © 1972 by Edwin Brock. Reprinted with permission of New Directions Publishing Corp.

"Returning to the World" © Barbara Carey. Reprinted by permission of Quarry Press Inc. from the anthology *Poets 88*.

"If a Tree Falls" © 1988 Golden Mountain Music Corp. Words and music by Bruce Cockburn. Taken from the album "Big Circumstance." Used by permission.

From "For E.J.P." by Leonard Cohen from *Flowers from Hitler* used by permission of the Canadian Publishers, McClelland & Stewart, Toronto. "For Anne" by Leonard Cohen from *Selected Poems* used by permission of the Canadian Publishers, McClelland & Stewart, Toronto.

"To a Fat Lady Seen from the Train," "A Recollection," and "Youth" by Frances Cornford from *Collected Poems* reprinted with permission of the Cresset Press.

"Stillborn" by Lorna Crozier reprinted with permission of the author.

''who knows if the moon's'' is reprinted from *Tulips & Chimneys* by E.E. Cummings, Edited by George James Firmage, by permission of Liveright Publishing Corporation. Copyright 1923, 1925 and renewed 1951, 1953 by E.E. Cummings. Copyright © 1973, 1976, by the Trustees for the E.E. Cummings Trust. Copyright © 1973, 1976 by George James Firmage. ''e'' is reprinted from *Complete Poems, 1913-1962,* by E.E. Cummings, by permission of Liveright Publishing Corporation. Copyright © 1923, 1925, 1931, 1935, 1938, 1939, 1940, 1944, 1945, 1946, 1947, 1948, 1949, 1950, 1951, 1952, 1953, 1954, 1955, 1956, 1957, 1958, 1959, 1960, 1961, 1962 by the Trustees for the E.E. Cummings Trust. Copyright © 1961, 1963, 1968 by Marion Morehouse Cummings.

''Waiting,'' ''Is It?'' and ''Spring's Miracle'' from *Grief: Climbing Toward Understanding* by Phyllis Davies. Copyright © 1988 by Phyllis Davies. Published by arrangement with Carol Publishing Group. A Lyle Stuart Book.

''Wild Geese'' by Joyce Davis from *English Journal* (May 1977). Copyright 1977 by the National Council of Teachers of English. Reprinted with permission.

''As in the Beginning'' by Mary di Michele is reprinted from *Necessary Sugar* by permission of Oberon Press.

''Seeing Myself on TV'' by Leona Dubay from *English Journal* (May 1977). Copyright 1977 National Council of Teachers of English. Reprinted with permission.

''Seven Days'' by Gary Dunford reprinted with permission of the author.

''This Fevers Me'' by Richard Eberhart reprinted with permission of the author.

*''Desiderata'' by M. Ehrmann (see p. 242)

''Progress?'' by Hubert Evans from the anthology *The Seasons of Children* (Simon & Pierre) reprinted with permission of the literary estate of Hubert Evans, Elizabeth Bakewell.

''The Philosophers'' by R.G. Everson has been reprinted by permission of Oberon Press. ''L'Original'' by R.G. Everson is reprinted from *Everson at 80* by permission of Oberon Press.

''The Night Will Never Stay'' by Eleanor Farjeon from *Poems for Children*. Reprinted by permission of Harold Ober Associates Inc. Copyright © 1951 by Eleanor Farjeon.

''To the Friend I Broke Up With'' by Lynne Ferguson from *English Journal* (May 1977). Copyright 1977 by the National Council of Teachers of English. Reprinted with permission.

''The World Is A Beautiful Place'' by Lawrence Ferlinghetti from *A Coney Island of the Mind*. Copyright © 1958 by Lawrence Ferlinghetti. Reprinted with permission of New Directions Publishing Corp.

''Poem for My Father'' by Owen Fitzhugh from *English Journal* (December 1987). Copyright 1987 by the National Council of Teachers of English. Reprinted with permission.

''Empty Holds a Question'' by Pat Folk reprinted with permission of the author.

Excerpt from *Anne Frank: The Diary of a Young Girl* by Anne Frank, copyright 1952 by Otto H. Frank. Used by permission of Doubleday, a division of Bantam Doubleday Dell Publishing Group, Inc.

''Nothing Gold Can Stay,'' ''Take Something Like a Star,'' ''Stopping by Woods on a Snowy Evening,'' and the excerpt from ''The Pasture'' from *The Poetry of Robert Frost* edited by Edward Connery Lathem. Copyright 1916, 1923, 1939, © 1967, 1969 by Holt, Rinehart and Winston. Copyright 1944, 1951 by Robert Frost. Reprinted by permission of Henry Holt and Company, Inc.

''Credo'' by Robert Fulghum from *All I Really Need to Know I Learned in Kindergarten* by Robert Fulghum. Copyright © 1986, 1988 by Robert Fulghum. Reprinted by permission of Villard Books, a division of Random House Inc.

''The Drum'' by Nikki Giovanni from *Spin a Soft Black Song*. Copyright © 1971, 1985 by Nikki Giovanni. Reprinted by permission of Farrar, Straus and Giroux, Inc.

''Passing Words'' by Susan Glickman from *Complicity* (Signal Editions, Véhicule Press) reprinted with permission of Véhicule Press.

''Justice,'' and ''Terry'' by Leona Gom from *Northbound* (Thistledown Press) reprinted with permission of the author.

Excerpt from ''This One's On Me,'' and ''First Person Demonstrative'' by Phyllis Gotlieb reprinted with permission of the author.

''Bonsai, Haiku, a Seashell'' by Elizabeth Gourlay reprinted with permission of the author.

"A Dark Thing Inside the Day" by Linda Gregg from *American Poetry Review* 17, 4 reprinted with permission of the author.

"Here Comes the Sun" by George Harrison © 1969 HARRISONGS LTD. International Copyright Secured. All Rights Reserved.

"Living Is," and "Making Sense" by Piet Hein from *Grook* reprinted with permission of Piet Hein Ltd., Denmark.

"Return" by David Helwig is reprinted from *The Sign of the Gunman* by permission of Oberon Press.

"Today As I Passed Through the Market-Place" by Robert Hillyer. Copyright 1933 and renewed 1961 by Robert Hillyer. Reprinted by permission of Alfred A. Knopf Inc.

"Stupidity Street" by Ralph Hodgson from *Selected Poems* (Macmillan, London and Basingstoke) reprinted with permission of Macmillan London.

"Conversation with a Poet" by Miroslav Holub translated by Ewald Osers reprinted by permission of Bloodaxe Books Ltd. from *Poems: Before and After* by Miroslav Holub (Bloodaxe Books, 1990).

"Florida Road Workers" by Langston Hughes from *The Panther and the Lash*. Copyright © 1967 by Langston Hughes. Reprinted by permission of Alfred A. Knopf Inc.

"Untitled" © 1969 by David Ignatow reprinted from *Poems 1934-1969* by permission of University Press of New England. First appeared in *The Nation*.

"The World of Dew" by Kobayishi Issa from *The Penguin Book of Japanese Verse* translated by Geoffrey Bownas and Anthony Thwaite (Penguin Books, 1964), copyright © Geoffrey Bownas and Anthony Thwaite, 1964.

"June Bug" by Pat Jasper from *Recycling* (Fiddlehead Poetry Books & Goose Lane Editions, 1985). Used with permission of Goose Lane Editions, Fredericton, New Brunswick.

"Losings" by Suzanne Jay from *English Journal* (October 1987). Copyright 1987 by the National Council of Teachers of English. Reprinted with permission.

"Deforestation" by Scott Keedwell reprinted with permission of the author.

"Keep a Hand on Your Dream" by X.J. Kennedy from *Poetspeak* edited by Paul B. Janeczko (Bradbury Press). Copyright © 1983 by X.J. Kennedy. Reprinted with permission of the author.

"Furrows" by Debbie Phillips Kuhnley from *English Journal* (March 1988). Copyright 1988 by the National Council of Teachers of English. Reprinted with permission.

"Your Country" ("Ton Pays") by Gatien Lapointe found in *The Poetry of French Canada in Translation* (Oxford University Press) reprinted with permission of the literary estate of Gatien Lapointe.

"Refutation" by Irving Layton from *Lovers and Lesser Men*. Used by permission of the Canadian Publishers, McClelland & Stewart, Toronto.
"Innocence" by Irving Layton from *The Collected Poems of Irving Layton*. Used by permission of the Canadian Publishers, McClelland & Stewart, Toronto.

"What Will You Be?" by Dennis Lee from *Garbage Delight* © 1977 by Dennis Lee. Reprinted by permission of Macmillan of Canada, A Division of Canada Publishing Corporation. Excerpt from "Nicholas Knock" by Dennis Lee from *Nicholas Knock and Other People* by Dennis Lee, published by Macmillan of Canada, with the permission of the author.

"A Coffin and a Chevy" by Carl Leggo first published in *Voices* (April 1989) and then in *The New Quarterly* 9, 3 (Fall 1989). Reprinted with the permission of the author.

"The Big Years" by Jo Lena reprinted with permission of the author.

"The Secret" and "Psalm Concerning the Castle" by Denise Levertov from *Poems 1960-1967*. Copyright © 1964, 1966 by Denise Levertov Goodman. "Epilogue" by Denise Levertov from *Life in the Forest*. Copyright © 1978 by Denise Levertov. Reprinted with permission of New Directions Publishing Corp.

"I Thought I Saw Stars" by R.P. Lister reprinted by permission of *Punch*.

"What Is the Validity of Your Life," "The Difference" and "Pioneer" by Dorothy Livesay from *Collected Poems: The Two Seasons* (Fitzhenry & Whiteside) reprinted with permission of the author.

"Rumours of War" by Pat Lowther from *A Stone Diary* by Pat Lowther, © Oxford University Press Canada 1977; reprinted by permission of the publisher.

"Leonardo" by Nellie McClung from *Baraka: The Poems of Nellie McClung* (Intermedia, 1978) reprinted with permission of the author.

"Assignment: Poetry" by Kayla L. McClurg from *English Journal* (December 1987). Copyright 1987 by the National Council of Teachers of English. Reprinted with permission.

"Second Degree Burns," "Fire Gardens," "Flight One," "The Compass," and "Letter to a Future Generation" by Gwendolyn MacEwen reprinted with permission of the estate of Gwendolyn MacEwen.

"A True Poem" by David McFadden from *Intense Pleasure* used by permission of the Canadian Publishers, McClelland & Stewart, Toronto.

"Memory from Childhood" by Antonio Machado translated by Robert Bly from *The Massachusetts Review* 14, 4 (1974). Reprinted from *The Massachusetts Review* © 1974, The Massachusetts Review Inc. with permission.

"Reading Poetry" by Mary McIver from *English Journal* (December 1988). Copyright 1988 by the National Council of Teachers of English. Reprinted with permission.

"If We Must Die" by Claude McKay from *Selected Poems of Claude McKay* (Twayne) copyright 1953 and reprinted with the permission of Twayne Publishers, a division of G.K. Hall & Co. Boston.

"Lone Dog" by Irene Rutherford McLeod from *Songs to Save a Soul* (Chatto & Windus). Reprinted with permission of Random Century Group.

"Remembrance" by Alice Major reprinted with permission of the author.

"I Know," and "Forget It" by Carolyn Mamchur reprinted with permission of the author.

"Lesson of the Moth" by Don Marquis excerpted from *Archy and Mehitabel* by Don Marquis, copyright 1927 by Doubleday, a division of Bantam, Doubleday, Dell Publishing Group Inc. Used by permission of the publisher.

"Lucinda Matlock" by Edgar Lee Masters from *Spoon River Anthology* (Macmillan) reprinted with permission of the literary estate of Edgar Lee Masters.

"Springsong" by Robin Mathews from *Language of Fire* (Steel Rail Publishing, 1976) reprinted with permission of the author.

"Metaphor" by Eve Merriam from *A Sky Full of Poems*. Copyright © 1964, 1970, 1973 by Eve Merriam; "Fee, Fi, Fo, Fum" from *The Inner City Mother Goose* by Eve Merriam. Copyright © 1969, 1982 by Eve Merriam. "Fantasia" from *Finding a Poem* by Eve Merriam. Copyright © 1970 by Eve Merriam. Reprinted by permission of Marian Reiner for the author.

Excerpt from "A Few Figs from Thistles," and "Lament" by Edna St. Vincent Millay from *Collected Poems* (Harper & Row). Copyright 1921, 1922, 1948, 1950 by Edna St. Vincent Millay. Reprinted by permission of Elizabeth Barnett, Literary Executor. "Apostrophe to Man" by Edna St. Vincent Millay from *Collected Poems*. Copyright © 1934, 1962 by Edna St. Vincent Millay and Norma Millay Ellis. Reprinted by permission of Elizabeth Barnett, Literary Executor.

"I Fell (Vers Libre)" by Lucy Maud Montgomery from *The Poetry of Lucy Maud Montgomery* (Fitzhenry & Whiteside) reprinted with permission.

"Strawberries" by Edwin Morgan from *Poems of Thirty Years* (Carcanet Press) reprinted with permission.

"Listen, Real Poetry Doesn't Say Anything" by Jim Morrison from *Wilderness*. Copyright © 1988 by Columbus Courson and Pearl Courson. Reprinted by permission of Villard Books, a division of Random House, Inc.

"Seaside Serenade" by Ogden Nash from *Verses from 1929 On* (Little, Brown and Company) reprinted with permission. First appeared in *The Saturday Evening Post*.

"To David, About His Education" by Howard Nemerov from *The Collected Poems of Howard Nemerov* (University of Chicago Press, 1977). Reprinted by permission of the author.

"Complaining Day" by Mary Neville from *Woody and Me* by Mary Neville. Copyright © 1966 by Mary Neville Woodrich. Reprinted by permission of Pantheon Books, a division of Random House, Inc.

"When I Heard of the Friend's Death" by John Newlove from *Black Night Window* (McClelland & Stewart, 1968) reprinted with permission of the author.

"Prayer" by bp Nichol reprinted with permission.

"Greatness" by Alden Nowlan from *The Mysterious Naked Man* (Clarke, Irwin, 1969) reprinted with permission of Stoddart Publishing Co. "The Fynch Cows" by Alden Nowlan from *Under the Ice* (Ryerson, 1961) reprinted with permission of Claudine Nowlan, Literary Executors.

"A Heart That Has Been Broken" by Maureen Owen reprinted with permission of the author.

"Dulce et Decorum Est" by Wilfred Owen from *Wilfred Owen: The Complete Poems and Fragments* edited by Jon Stallworthy (Hogarth Press) reprinted with permission of the Estate of Wilfred Owen and Random Century Group.

"Stefan," "A Backwards Journey," "Adolescence," and "Star-Gazer" by P.K. Page reprinted with permission of the author.

"The Five Stages of Grief" is reprinted from *The Five Stages of Grief*, poems by Linda Pastan, by permission of W.W. Norton & Company, Inc. Copyright © 1978 by Linda Pastan.

"Erosion" by E.J. Pratt from *E.J. Pratt: Complete Poems* Vol. 1 edited by Sandra Djwa and R.G. Mayles. Reprinted with permission of University of Toronto Press.

"And This Is Love" by Paula Reingold from *Etc* 22, 2 reprinted by permission of the International Society for General Semantics, San Francisco.

"Disillusionment" by Gayle Reynolds from *English Journal* (May 1977). Copyright 1977 by the National Council of Teachers of English. Reprinted with permission.

"Motionless Swaying" by Yannis Ritsos from *Gestures and Other Poems* translated by Nikos Stangos (Jonathan Cape) reprinted with permission of Random Century Group.

"Foreign Student" by Barbara Robinson from *English Journal* (May 1976). Copyright 1976 by the National Council of Teachers of English. Reprinted with permission.

"Reuben Bright" by Edwin Arlington Robinson from *The Children of the Night* (New York: Charles Scribner's Sons, 1897).

"I Get High on Butterflies" by Joe Rosenblatt from *Top Sail* (Porcépic Books) reprinted with permission.

"Pterodactyls" by Marjoree L. Sallee from *English Journal* (September 1987). Copyright 1987 by the National Council of Teachers of English. Reprinted with permission.

Excerpt from "Tentative Definitions of Poetry" by Carl Sandburg from *Good Morning America*, copyright 1928 and renewed 1956 by Carl Sandburg, reprinted by permission of Harcourt Brace Jovanovich, Inc.

"Occupation" by Pat Sargent from *English Journal* (May 1975). Copyright 1975 by the National Council of Teachers of English. Reprinted with permission.

"Question" by Chris Sawotin reprinted by permission of the author.

"New Names" by F.R. Scott from *The Collected Poems of F.R. Scott*. Used by permission of the Canadian Publishers, McClelland & Stewart, Toronto.

"Lament" by Anne Sexton from *All My Pretty Ones*. Copyright © 1962 by Anne Sexton. Reprinted by permission of Houghton Mifflin Co.

"Invitation" by Shel Silverstein from *Where the Sidewalk Ends*. Copyright © 1974 by Evil Eye Music, Inc. Reprinted with permission of Harper-Collins Publishers.

"How Beautifully Useless" by Raymond Souster is reprinted from *The Eyes of Love* by permission of Oberon Press. "The Lilac Poem," and "City Hall Street" by Raymond Souster from *Collected Poems of Raymond Souster* reprinted by permission of Oberon Press.

"Empty House" by Stephen Spender from *The Edge of Being* reprinted with permission of Faber and Faber Limited, London.

"Lament" by Jon Stallworthy © Oxford University Press 1961. Reprinted from *The Astronomy of Love* by Jon Stallworthy (1961) by permission of Oxford University Press.

"I Sought All Over the World" by John Tagliabue from *Poems*. Copyright 1954, 1955, 1956, 1957, 1958, 1959 by John Tagliabue. Reprinted by permission of HarperCollins Publishers.

"Barter" by Sara Teasdale from *Collected Poems*. Reprinted with permission of Macmillan Publishing Company. Copyright 1917 by Macmillan Publishing Company, renewed 1945 by Mamie T. Wheless. "There Will Come Soft Rains" by Sara Teasdale from *Collected Poems* (Macmillan, 1937).

"Fern Hill" by Dylan Thomas from *The Poems* (Dent). Reprinted with permission of David Higham Associates, London.

"Planting" by Yvonne Trainer from the anthology *Poets 88* (Quarry Press) reprinted by permission of Quarry Press Inc. "Night" by Yvonne Trainer from *Everything Happens at Once* by Yvonne Trainer (Goose Lane Editions, 1986). Reprinted with the permission of the publisher.

"You're Grounded!" by Lidia Tremblay from *And Other Travels* (Moonstone Press) reprinted with permission of the publisher.

"Advice to the Young" by Miriam Waddington from *Collected Poems*, © Miriam Waddington 1986; reprinted by permission of Oxford University Press Canada.

"Alba" by Derek Walcott from *In a Green Night: 1948-1960*. Copyright © 1962 by Derek Walcott. Reprinted by permission of Farrar, Straus and Giroux, Inc.

"Good Night Willie Lee, I'll See You in the Morning" copyright © 1975 by Alice Walker. From *Good Night Willie Lee, I'll See You in the Morning* by Alice Walker. Used by permission of Doubleday, a division of Bantam Doubleday Dell Publishing Group Inc.

"Common Magic" by Bronwen Wallace from *Common Magic* reprinted with permission of Oberon Press.

"Vimy Unveiling" by Joe Wallace from *Poems* (Progress Books, 1981) reprinted with the permission of the publisher.

"Students" by Tom Wayman from *The Face of Jack Monroe* (Harbour Publishing) reprinted with permission of the publisher.

"Alex" by Phyllis Webb from *Selected Poems 1954-1965* (Talon Books, 1971) reprinted with permission of the author.

"The Pardon" by Richard Wilbur from *Ceremony and Other Poems*, copyright 1950 and renewed 1978 by Richard Wilbur, reprinted by permission of Harcourt Brace Jovanovich Inc.

"The Act" by William Carlos Williams from *The Collected Poems of William Carlos Williams, 1939-1962, Vol. II*. Copyright 1948 by William Carlos Williams. "A Young Woman at a Window," and "Thursday" by William Carlos Williams from *The Collected Poems of William Carlos Williams, 1909-1939, Vol. I*. Copyright 1938 by New Directions Publishing Corporation. Reprinted with permission of New Directions Publishing Corporation.

"Ascent" by Adele Wiseman first published in *Poetry by Canadian Women* (Oxford University Press) reprinted with permission of the author.

"The Frost" by Tzu Yeh from *An Introduction to Haiku* edited by Harold G. Henderson, copyright © 1958 by Harold G. Henderson. Used by permission of Doubleday, a division of Bantam Doubleday Dell Publishing Group Inc.

"Lies" by Yevgeny Yevtushenko from *Yevtushenko: Selected Poems* translated by Robin Milner-Gulland and Peter Levi, S.J. (Penguin Books, 1962), copyright © Robin Milner-Gulland and Peter Levi, 1962.

"Lester Tells of Wanda and the Big Snow" by Paul Zimmer from *With Wanda: Town and Country Poems* © 1980 by Paul Zimmer, published by Dryad Press. Reprinted with permission. "What Zimmer Would Be" by Paul Zimmer from *The Zimmer Poems* © 1976 by Paul Zimmer, published by Dryad Press. Reprinted with permission.

"Computer Report Card" by Meguido Zola reprinted with permission of the author.

*"The Desiderata of Happiness" by Max Ehrmann ©1927 by M. Ehrmann. All rights reserved. Copyright renewed 1954 by B. Ehrmann. Reprinted by permission of Robert L. Bell, Melrose, MA 02176 USA